The Student's Guide
to
London

The Student's Guide
to
London

by

Larry Lain and Jeff Griffin

University of Dayton
Dayton, Ohio

Illustrations by
Ewa Pietroczuk

The McDonald & Woodward Publishing Company
Blacksburg, Virginia
1998

The McDonald & Woodward Publishing Company
P. O. Box 10308, Blacksburg, Virginia 24060

The Student's Guide to London

All rights reserved. First Printing August 1998
Printed in the United States of America by
McNaughton & Gunn, Inc., Saline, Michigan

04 03 02 01 00 99 98   10 9 8 7 6 5 4 3 2 1

Library of Congress Cataloging-in-Publication Data

Lain, Larry, 1947–
    The student's guide to London / by Larry Lain and Jeff
Griffin ; illustrations by Ewa Pietroczuk.
        p.   cm.
    Includes index.
    ISBN 0–939923–80–7 (pbk. : alk. paper)
    1. Foreign study--England--London--Handbooks, manu-
als, etc. 2. Students, Foreign--England--London--
Handbooks, manuals, etc. 3. London (England)--
Guidebooks. I. Griffin, Jeff, 1957–   . II. Title.
LB2376.3.G7L35   1998
914.204'859--dc21   98–28147
                                                      CIP

Contents

PART I
QUESTIONS AND ANSWERS

Acknowledgments

Practically everyone we know has helped with this project in some way, whether with information, ideas, advice, or just encouragement. If we listed them all, the book would be so large you couldn't afford to buy it! We'd like to mention a few very special people, however, beginning with our wonderful wives Barb and Ewa (who is also our talented illustrator), without whom nothing else is possible.

We've received countless ideas from our own students in the University of Dayton's London Communication program over the years, as well as support, both moral and financial, from UD's office of International Educational Programs.

We'd also like to give special mention to some of the many people in London whose ideas and assistance turn up in the pages that follow. Contributors to the Usenet group *rec.travel.europe* include T. Backus, Martin Drew, Michael J. Gallagher, Alycia Weinberger, and the ever kind and thoughtful Ben Haines. Also due special mention are Sandra Cumming of the Royal Society, Kate Davey and Elizabeth Graham of the Wellcome Centre for Medical Science, Professor David Edwards of Imperial College, Dr. Roland Jackson of the Science Museum, Dr. John Johnston of the Royal Society of Chemistry, Anne McCartney of the London Transport Museum, and Martin Rich of City University. And we offer a warm thanks to our favorite publicans, David and Lisa Scully of the Lord John Russell, for their advice, their friendship, and their beer.

The Student's Guide
to
London

Introduction

You're serving an academic sentence of 10 to 15 years, time spent sitting in one classroom or the other, listening to Dr. Monotone or Professor Drivel inform you about trickle-down economics or the migratory nature of swallows or life on Mars or whatever. Sometimes the walls seem like they're going to close in on you. Even if you are blessed with the best and brightest of teachers — and we know *our* students are! — education can fail to excite.

What you need is time off for good behavior. A stint abroad will put the luster back in learning. That's because study abroad is — or at least *ought to be* — a vastly different educational experience. You are in another country, and an inexhaustible supply of cultural resources can irrigate the seeds of learning.

In the first half of this book, we're going to convince you that your education won't be complete unless you go to London for a summer, semester, year, or any chunk you can carve time into. We'll help you figure out how to make your dream a reality. We'll help you prepare for your study sojourn by guiding you as you choose a program, figure out how you're going to pay for it, and go about informing yourself about the sceptered isle. We'll tell you what to do once you get off the plane — or whatever other form of transportation brought you to England — and help you orient yourself to your new environment.

The second half of the book is dedicated to insider tips on having a *fun* and multifaceted educational experience in London. We look at London's offerings subject by subject, pointing out the enriching experiences, the wondrous walks, the out-of-the-way places that can bring to life the fields you are studying or are otherwise interested in. We believe learning can be an adventure, and we put great stock in exploration and self-discovery. This book doesn't tell you that this place or that is the best, the number one, the see-at-all-costs site. We don't bother rating sites with *x* number of stars or miniature Tower Bridge icons or Shakespeare busts. (You'll find a different kind of bust on page 3 in London's biggest-selling daily newspaper, *The Sun*!) What's four stars to us may be only two to you. Instead, this book aims to whet your appetite for creating a unique, individualized London experience that goes far beyond that of the casual visitor. We help you figure out how to absorb the essence of London — *your* London — not a tour guide's or your teacher's. Turn the page and fasten your seatbelt. You're on your way to London!

Part I

Questions and Answers

If you're thinking, however casually, about the possibility of foreign study, you have a lot of questions. That's why we're here. Foreign study is something we believe in wholeheartedly, and we want to do everything we can to make it possible for you to pursue this experience. We've been involved in foreign-study programs for years, and we think we know many of the questions and concerns you have.

The first seven chapters of the book will answer fundamental questions most students have about foreign study in general and studying in London in particular. They can help you make up your mind if such an experience is something you'll benefit from, and they may also be able to help persuade your parents to give their blessing to your trip.

Ready? Then let's tackle those questions!

Chapter 1

Why Would I Want To Leave a Perfectly Comfortable Home and Study in Some Foreign Country?

We're teachers and writers, so we don't deal in cliches. We are not going to tell you that *the world is getting smaller every day*. It's not. The world is still about 25,000 miles around — a little over 40,000 kilometers, if you prefer — and a bit less than 8000 miles, or 13,000 kilometers, through the middle. It hasn't changed much, and it would be big headlines if it did . . . if any of us were still alive to read them!

What *is* true is that modern means of trans-portation and communication have allowed all the world's people to interact with one another more than at any time in history — whether they like it or not — and the frequency of those interactions is escalating constantly. Most of us do not come into *daily* contact with people from other countries, either face-to-face or through some less personal way of communicating, nor do we go jetting off to foreign shores routinely.

But that time *is* coming.

Fifty years ago it was unusual for people to travel much beyond a day's journey from their homes, except for special occasions, natural disasters, or war. Frankly, *our* parents have never understood why *we* are so enamored of travel. We spend good money for the dubious pleasure of sitting for hours trapped in a tin can with wings, trying to get somewhere that doesn't get our TV shows, and going to places where people can't understand plain English.

Why go to all that trouble?

Because the 21st century is going to be very different from the ones that came before it. Consider the following. Western Europe, once a bastion of nationalism, has formed an economic union that has increased contact and cooperation among nations in unprecedented ways. The United States, often isolationist and aloof (except militarily), sends hundreds of thousands of tourists abroad annually. Asian business interests have increased contact and travel between East and West to levels that would have been hard to imagine just a few years ago. Even the former Soviet bloc has opened welcoming arms to the rest of the world.

Here's an amazing fact that your history-major friends can confirm: there is now more change *every single year* than took place in the entire world during the *one thousand years* between the years 500 to 1500. And this, friends, is the world you are going to spend the rest of your lives in. You do not even want to think about how much of what you're learning in school and paying tuition for will be obsolete 10 years from now.

In part, money is driving all this change. Europe realized that to be competitive in world trade with North America and the Far East, it would have to put aside many long-nurtured differences. A strong economy in America has given record numbers of people the means of traveling to places they'd only seen on television. Asian automobiles and electronics have claimed worldwide markets from other countries. And the newly capitalistic nations of Eastern Europe are trying to catch up with the economics of the rest of the world.

Technology plays big a role, too. Can you imagine crossing an ocean by rocking and pitching and tossing (erp!) for a month in a sailing ship? Or crossing a continent by bouncing along rutted roads in a wagon, knowing there could be a highwayman behind any rock? Or crossing either in a groaning and creaking, underpowered propeller-driven airplane that flies *through* the storms and weather fronts instead of miles *above* them? Those were the choices earlier generations had for long-distance travel. No wonder they stayed home!

You know more about the rest of the world than any generation in human history.

9

- You routinely watch television broadcast live from thousands of miles away.
- Your newspaper carries color photographs of events that took place across the ocean just hours earlier.
- You can talk on the telephone with a friend 10,000 miles away and hear her like she was in the next room, all for a fraction of what it used to cost.
- Through the Internet you can read today's newspaper or listen to the radio from dozens of countries.
- You can look up information in libraries in London or Washington or Berlin from your desktop computer faster than you can walk across campus to your own library.
- You can instantly exchange e-mail messages with people almost anywhere in the world for free.

And the changes that will come during your working life will make these seem trivial.

It used to be that a "good education" meant that you studied Latin and Greek, philosophy and astrology. That was about it. Our definitions of what constitutes a "good education" have changed radically over the centuries. Taken any good astrology classes lately? (No, we are not asking *What's your sign* . . . .) A couple of generations ago, a simple liberal-arts education was considered suitable for everyone. Then professional schools like business and engineering came to the forefront. Social sciences began matching, then surpassing, humanities in majors. We are in an age of specialization, both educationally and occupationally. The more marketable knowledge and experience you have, the more valuable you are going to be to a prospective employer.

Which brings us back to the value of studying abroad. Precisely *because* of the incredible ease of international transportation and communication and the growing desire of businesses to market themselves globally, people in just about *any* field (except, possibly, astrology) who have sound international experience are much more valuable than at any time in the past.

The applications of this are obvious in business and technology, but they are true in countless other areas as well. Natural scientists have always been an international community. There is, in fields like education and social science, an increasing emphasis on the understanding of the diverse cultures that make up the world, something the folks in the humanities had always been sensitive to. You are far more likely to travel internationally than your parents were as part of your career, because modern times demand it.

A personal example: the brother-in-law of one of the authors spent his life in a midwestern United States city; he even went to college there. Within two years after he completed graduate school, his very first employer had sent him to at least four European countries. He now travels abroad several times a year.

Having a foreign-study experience on your resume shows prospective employers that you are probably a person who thinks globally, who is adaptable and embraces new experiences, who learns quickly, and who

11

can cope with the unexpected. Those are exactly the qualities employers value in the people who work for them!

But forget about jobs, money, and success! (We know you won't forget about them and your parents certainly don't want you to, but try for a moment.) There is another reason to study abroad.

The world is filled with things you know little about — but should. If you are going to be a citizen of the world, as we all must be in years to come, you have to get at least a sense of the marvelous variety of humanity the world offers. From infancy, in almost every culture, we are taught to look for the ways in which other people are different from us — different skin, different religion, different clothing, different language, and different customs. The list of differences is overwhelming.

But *different* doesn't mean *worse*. It just means something we're not used to. Maybe eating raw fish isn't your cup of tea. But it's a wonderful staple of daily life to countless people. Perhaps you find squat toilets odd and embarrassing. A billion people use them every day. A *billion!* Is baseball too boring or mystifyingly complicated for you? Hundreds of millions of North and South Americans watch and play the game all summer long.

The point is, *your* way of doing things is not the only way. You will function far better as a citizen of the world if you have a sense of your own place in it and how to interact with all those people who are different from you.

Learning and appreciating the *differences* among people is only half the reason for studying abroad, however. Just as important is to come to a realization of how much *alike* we all are. We've seen lovers walking down the street in places from Montreal to Moscow, holding hands in the same way. We've seen children teasing their parents, hiding behind trees in the park and jumping out at them. They jump and shout and giggle in exactly the same way in London and in Chicago. We've seen students prowling through bookshops, looking for the same kinds of bargains in a dozen countries. If you couldn't hear the language or see the signs, you couldn't tell whether the student was Israeli, Nigerian, or Thai.

People of every nationality and creed stop to stare in just the same way at a brilliant sunset, rail as adamantly against the same kinds of injustice, and share the same smile with strangers at the antics of squirrels chasing each other around a tree. To realize these things intellectually is one thing. To see them, to live them, to *know* them is something altogether more moving.

So why should you go abroad to *study*? Can't you get just as much from being a tourist? Frankly — no.

Tourists are passing through. They are largely insulated from the deeper culture of the country they're visiting. Most of the time they stay in hotels quite unlike the homes of the people around them. They go to the big tourist attractions and eat in restaurants that cater to tourists. At worst they are herded into air-conditioned buses and driven directly to a series of attractions. A foreign city becomes just a theme park, and the people merely exhibits and actors.

To *study* abroad, though, is to live a life closer to that of your host country. You'll find local hangouts away from the tourist tracks. You'll meet local students and neighborhood residents eating in the little restaurants the tourists never go near, having a *cafe au lait* in the morning outside a bistro a mile from the nearest tour bus, or reading the local morning newspaper.

Whether you stay for two weeks or six months, you feel more a part of your city as a student because you're *living* there, not just visiting. The psychological and practical differences are enormous.

Of course you won't ignore the big attractions. Why would you go to Rome and not see St. Peter's or to London and miss the Tower? But as a student you have an excuse to visit the places that are more closely associated with what you're studying, even if they're not included in all the famous guidebooks.

Our mission here is to take you to London, one of the world's great cities and one of the chief cities in the world for students to visit. In the pages to come, we'll

show you some of the things we think you'll be interested in — more than enough to get you started. London is too big and too complex for us to cover *every* interesting sight in *every* discipline. But our suggestions will take you places you might never find otherwise and encourage you to seek out more on your own.

Studying in London, whether for a few weeks or for several months, will change you forever. You'll never look at yourself or at the world in the same way again. You'll acquire knowledge about your field of study, you'll grow as a person, you'll become confident about things you never dreamed existed just months earlier, and you'll be better prepared to take this new You out into the rest of your life.

A final note. Parents are sometimes reluctant to see their children, no matter how old they are, trotting off to foreign lands. Let *them* read this book, too. We think we can help you make your best case for going. In fact, we hope we just did!

Chapter 2

Why Would I Want To Study in London?

Studying abroad exhilarates. For the first week — perhaps every week — you'll feel as though you're several feet off the ground because everything around you is different and exciting. You won't be in Carbondale, Chapel Hill, Cincinnati, Corvallis, or wherever your school is located. Instead, you'll be in another country!

Studying abroad is wonderful, no matter where. But we can make a fine case for studying in London.

Multifaceted and vibrant, London has something for everyone. For students of literature, this is the land of Charles Dickens, Lord Byron, Daniel Defoe, Jane Austen, Thomas Hardy, and Evelyn Waugh, just to scratch the surface. On the London stage, you can see Shakespearean works in a variety of settings, including the rebuilt Globe Theatre. The diverse London theatre scene encompasses musicals such as Andrew Lloyd Webber's *Cats* or *Sunset Boulevard* or Alain Boublil and Claude-Michel Schonberg's *Les Miserables*. Farcical comedies and searing dramas also have a home on the London stage. Daring, convention-defying productions are often found on the fringe-theatre scene.

The history student's heart must beat fast at the thought of Boudicca, Julius Caesar, William the Conqueror, Henry VIII, Margaret Thatcher — leaders who left an indelible imprint on London. The Tower of London and Westminster Abbey are just two of the hundreds of London landmarks that cast a long historical shadow. The plague year, the Great Fire of 1666, night raids by the *Luftwaffe* during World War II — the history student is speared on the points of a time line.

The *Magna Carta* and the British parliamentary tradition beckon the student of political science. The lawyer-to-be sees the bewigged barristers of the Inns of Court not as a cultural anachronism but as the symbol of a legal system that has evolved over many centuries.

The communication student can compare the public-speaking styles of the fervent and the less-than-sane at Speakers' Corner in Hyde Park or consider the journalistic philosophies represented by the sensationalistic tabloid newspapers such as *The Sun* and the quality papers such as *The Times*. This is the home of the British Broadcasting Corporation, which launched the first regular television service in the world and continues to create both informative and entertaining television programs that touch people in an era of increased competition from commercial broadcasters.

The hearts of science and engineering students ought to pound at the idea of studying in the city of Newton, of Darwin, and of Fleming. This is the city where the first subway trains ran beneath the earth's surface, where the first true computer was built, and where television made its debut.

Students of architecture will find buildings adored and buildings reviled, buildings of every era and buildings of every style. There's everything from the White Tower, a part of the Tower of London dating to the 11th century, to the grimly futuristic Lloyds of London, built some 900 years later. London is an architectural hodgepodge not predominantly characterized by a pervasive style in the way that Florence is defined by the 15th century, Paris by the 19th century, or Manhattan by the 20th.

Music students can attend performances by musicians considered among the finest in the world — as well as performances by those aspiring to be — at a wide variety of venues, ranging from St. Martin-in-the-Fields Church to Wigmore Hall to Ronnie Scott's jazz club.

No matter your field, London has a world-class museum that will enable you to step out of the classroom for some up-close reflection. Few other cities — if any — can boast of such an array of museums. Fine-arts museums such as the National Gallery and the Tate Gallery contain astonishingly rich collections. Museums of applied art range from the gargantuan Victoria and Albert to the more modest spaces of the William Morris Gallery. Students of the stage can visit the Shakespeare

Globe Museum, while those more attuned to the screen have the Museum of the Moving Image. The British Museum contains the artifacts of bygone civilizations. You could name any field, and there's a London museum or two or three lending insight to it. For students of the body, there's the Florence Nightingale Museum, while for students of the mind, there's the Freud Museum. The Imperial War Museum, the Guards Museum, and the Wellington Museum are just three of the many museums with resonance for history students. Did we miss your field with our small sampling of London's museums? Perhaps, but the point remains that London has a museum for you.

Let's not overlook the greatest museum of them all — London itself. This vibrant city is no dusty memorial to a civilization gone by. London is a bustling capital that is not only the heart of England but one of the most important cities in Europe and the world, by al-

most any measure. London is a crossroads of communication, finance, fashion, fine arts, and music. Studying in London goes beyond the classroom. It even goes beyond the museums and renowned sites of historical or contemporary interest. London's lure is enhanced by the work going on in its offices, by the art being created, by the life on the streets, and by the charm of its people. London is special in a way that words fail to adequately describe, so all the fine words in the world won't add up to London. London provides an incomparable pallet of colors for painting your study-abroad experience.

London is a dynamic place to work, to live, to play, or merely to visit. Those connections unveil different facets of London. Of course London doesn't change according to the infinitive, but the way you approach it and the way you perceive it vary.

Tourists take in Big Ben, the Tower of London, *Les Miserables*, a few pubs, and get back on the plane for Poughkeepsie. Business travelers may find themselves tethered to the City, heart of the financial district. By the way, the City of London is a specific area of London just north of the Thames River and east of the Borough of Holborn. Greater London is made up of 32 boroughs and the City of London, which is sometimes referred to as the Square Mile because of its compact size. With written communication, it's easy to distinguish between references to the City and the city and between the City of London and London. With spoken communication, this becomes a bit dodgier, so just be aware of the distinction and pay attention. People who live in London, like residents of any city, find them-

21

selves so immersed in daily life that many have never explored the relics of history or cornerstones of their own culture that attract the tourists.

Students enjoy a unique position. Your courses and your curiosity drive your explorations of London. You visit the places that the residents take for granted — sometimes more than once! We've met Londoners who pass by the Tower every day but have never been inside. What a shame! Tourists, on the other hand, fail to penetrate the veneer of the renowned and highly recommended. Usually tourists leave without any sense of culture, without any real sense of place — just a suitcase for the soul of discordant images and experiences that may add up to a good time but won't add up to London.

Being a student provides you with certain inherent advantages. For one thing, your professors, your courses, and your academic readings should help you begin to peel away layers of the onion that is London.

Typically students are in a foreign city for a longer period of time than tourists or business travelers. You may choose an intensive month-long program or perhaps you'll be in London for a semester or a whole year. A longer duration works to your advantage. You have the time to explore. Sometimes the lesser-known places or activities prove to be more wonderful and more memorable than the better-known ones. You have time to lose your preconceptions and expectations. You have time to be surprised. The surprise may be that you don't like the place or activity — that you don't connect to it. Oh well. Your next choice may spark cultural ecstasy.

When considering studying abroad, you have to take language into account. Unlike touring, studying in a foreign locale demands more of a visitor. For North Americans, London has the added advantage of the English language. Americans and Canadians can understand what Brits are saying with no trouble — well, *almost* no trouble. For many others, whether you are from Chile or Switzerland or Thailand, you may have studied English because of its ever-increasing role as a global language. English is the second language of choice for many people in many countries — it is useful for international travel and almost vital for international business.

Serious students must also consider what a city has to offer when they aren't consciously learning, doing, soaking up experiences related to their field of study. Fun! That's right. We're talking about letting your hair down and just having a ball. You can spend a sunny afternoon after class roller-blading in Hyde Park or smelling the flowers at Kew Gardens or trying to figure out the rules of cricket in a match at Lord's. You can discuss politics over a pint with a friendly Brit at a traditional pub. Sting or the Wallflowers or the Three Tenors may be playing at Wembley Stadium or the Royal Albert Hall while you're there. In need of sustenance for your soul? Go to Westminster Abbey, St. Pancras Church, or one of a hundred others on a Sunday morning. If you need to get the metropolis out of your system, trains can whisk you to such nearby destinations as Oxford, Cambridge, Canterbury, Bath, and Salisbury. But try as hard as you might, you'll never squeeze all the possibilities out of London. We know because we've tried, and our list of things to do and places to go gets *longer* after each visit. That's the true measure of a magnificent destination.

In London the learning never stops. Neither does the fun.

Chapter 3

Do I Have To Give Up a Year of My Life? What Kinds of Programs Are Available?

The last chapter has you so fired up about the idea of studying in London that notions are bouncing around like a pinball in your head. This would be a good time to elaborate on the types of opportunities that you'll find for study in London.

An exciting part of the study-abroad decision is narrowing the possibilities. We highly recommend that you dig around and explore those possibilities before making up your mind. To help you make your decision, consider the following key questions.

What do you want to study?

Perhaps you want to take courses in your major. Or maybe you want to step away from your major and explore other fields of study. There are academically specialized programs as well as broader, more general ones.

When would you like to go, and how long would you like to study abroad?

Some programs are offered in the fall term, some in the spring term, and some are offered over a full academic year. There are summer programs, and there are short-term programs.

Can you study through your own school and, if not, will your school give you academic credit for work done through another school or academic organization?

Most of you are considering studying in London as part of your college education. Some of you, however, may be high school students who want to seize the opportunity right away. High school students can skip to the end of the chapter, where we'll give you some pointers on finding a program.

College students have scores of choices. Your school may have its own London program led by professors from your campus. Perhaps your school has a membership in a consortium — an organization made up of member colleges — that operates a London program.

If your college doesn't have a direct involvement in a London program, don't despair. You can go on a program operated by another college or one offered by an organization that focuses on international-educational opportunities. You may opt to enroll directly at a London university that caters to international students or even a London university with a general student body.

The best place to start your information search would be at the international-programs office of your college. You can be advised by an expert on the myriad possibilities and, most likely, get the chance to look through comprehensive guides to study-abroad programs, such as the hefty *Peterson's Study Abroad* annual, as well as individual program brochures.

Study abroad is emphasized by so many colleges and universities that your school is likely to have an array of opportunities, and a London program may be one of them. If your college offers its own program in London, take a close look at it. Consider whether it suits your academic needs and weigh its reputation among students and faculty. Talk to people who have taken part in recent years. Studying abroad through a program sponsored by your school would almost certainly be the most convenient option. You won't have to jump through any hoops to figure out how the London study fits into your degree plans or what course credit you'll get. There's the added advantage of studying under professors whom you know or know of and of having some sense of teaching styles and expectations. Having convenient access to program administrators and faculty in the months before the program is a major plus. If you have financial-aid questions, you can get them answered on campus. There's also the post-program bonus of being able to reflect on your experiences in London with classmates and professors who were there with you.

An astounding number of colleges and universities offer programs of study in London, as a quick perusal of any study-abroad guidebook will prove. For example, *Peterson's Study Abroad* lists the following 48 institutions with London study programs:

AMERICAN UNIVERSITY (WASHINGTON, DC)
BEAVER COLLEGE (GLENSIDE, PA)
BOSTON UNIVERSITY (BOSTON, MA)
BUTLER UNIVERSITY (INDIANAPOLIS, IN)
CENTRAL COLLEGE (PELLA, IA)
COLBY COLLEGE (WATERVILLE, ME)
DREW UNIVERSITY (MADISON, NJ)
ECKERD COLLEGE (ST. PETERSBURG, FL)
FLORIDA STATE UNIVERSITY (TALLAHASSEE, FL)
HARDING UNIVERSITY (SEARCY, AZ)
HOLLINS COLLEGE (ROANOKE, VA)
ITHACA COLLEGE (ITHACA, NY)
JAMES MADISON UNIVERSITY (HARRISONBURG, VA)
MARYMOUNT COLLEGE-TARRYTOWN (TARRYTOWN, NY)
MARYMOUNT UNIVERSITY (ARLINGTON, VA)
MICHIGAN STATE UNIVERSITY (EAST LANSING, MI)
NORTHERN ILLINOIS UNIVERSITY (DEKALB, IL)
ROCKFORD COLLEGE (ROCKFORD, IL)
ROGER WILLIAMS UNIVERSITY (BRISTOL, RI)
ROSARY COLLEGE (RIVER FOREST, IL)
RUTGERS, THE STATE UNIVERSITY OF NEW JERSEY (NEW BRUNS-
    WICK, NJ)
ST. LAWRENCE UNIVERSITY (CANTON, NY)
SARAH LAWRENCE COLLEGE (BRONXVILLE, NY)
SCHILLER INTERNATIONAL UNIVERSITY (DUNEDIN, FL)
SOUTHWEST MISSOURI STATE UNIVERSITY (SPRINGFIELD, MO)
STATE UNIVERSITY OF NEW YORK (SUNY) AT BINGHAMTON (BING-
    HAMTON, NY)
SUNY AT NEW PALTZ (NEW PALTZ, NY)
SUNY AT OSWEGO (OSWEGO, NY)
SUNY AT BROCKPORT (BROCKPORT, NY)
SUNY COLLEGE AT CORTLAND (CORTLAND, NY) (Do you get the
    impression that SUNY puts a lot of emphasis on London study?)
SYRACUSE UNIVERSITY (SYRACUSE, NY)
TUFTS UNIVERSITY (MEDFORD, MA)

Hang on. We're not done yet. We can't forget about the University of This or That:

UNIVERSITY OF ARIZONA (TUCSON, AZ)
UNIVERSITY OF CONNECTICUT (STORRS, CT)
UNIVERSITY OF DELAWARE (NEWARK, DE)
UNIVERSITY OF HAWAII AT MANOA (HONOLULU, HI)
UNIVERSITY OF MARYLAND-COLLEGE PARK (COLLEGE PARK, MD)
UNIVERSITY OF MIAMI (CORAL GABLES, FL)
UNIVERSITY OF MINNESOTA (MINNEAPOLIS, MN)
UNIVERSITY OF NEW HAMPSHIRE (DURHAM, NH)
UNIVERSITY OF PITTSBURGH (PITTSBURGH, PA)
UNIVERSITY OF ROCHESTER (ROCHESTER, NY)
UNIVERSITY OF SOUTHERN MISSISSIPPI (HATTIESBURG, MS)
UNIVERSITY OF WISCONSIN-PLATTEVILLE (PLATTEVILLE, WI)
UNIVERSITY OF WISCONSIN-STEVENS POINT (STEVENS POINT, WI)
WEBSTER UNIVERSITY (ST. LOUIS, MO)
WHITWORTH COLLEGE (SPOKANE, WA)
YALE UNIVERSITY (NEW HAVEN, CT)

If your school doesn't have a London program, inquire whether it is a member of a consortium of universities with a London program. As we mentioned earlier, there are also programs sponsored by other types of academic organizations. *Peterson's* lists:

ACCENT INTERNATIONAL CONSORTIUM FOR ACADEMIC PROGRAMS ABROAD (MILWAUKEE, WI)
AMERICAN ASSOCIATION OF OVERSEAS STUDIES (NEW YORK, NY)
AMERICAN HERITAGE ASSOCIATION / NORTHWEST COUNCIL ON STUDY ABROAD (PORTLAND, OR)
AMERICAN INSTITUTE FOR FOREIGN STUDY (GREENWICH, CT)
COLLEGE CONSORTIUM FOR INTERNATIONAL STUDIES — ERIE COMMUNITY COLLEGE (BUFFALO, NY)
COLLEGE CONSORTIUM FOR INTERNATIONAL STUDIES (WASHINGTON, DC)
CONSORTIUM FOR INTERNATIONAL EDUCATION (IRVINE, CA)
INSTITUTE OF EUROPEAN STUDIES / INSTITUTE OF ASIAN STUDIES (CHICAGO, IL)

INTERSTUDY (MEDFORD, MA)
PARTNERSHIP FOR SERVICE-LEARNING (NEW YORK, NY)

You can also go directly through a college or university in London. Possibilities include:

AMERICAN COLLEGE IN LONDON
UNIVERSITY OF LONDON-GOLDSMITHS' COLLEGE
UNIVERSITY OF LONDON-KING'S COLLEGE
UNIVERSITY OF LONDON-LONDON SCHOOL OF ECONOMICS
UNIVERSITY OF LONDON-ROYAL HOLLOWAY COLLEGE
UNIVERSITY OF WESTMINSTER

Slap yourself. The point of bombarding you with names of colleges and organizations with programs was to open your eyes to the scads of possibilities. Believe it or not, the list of programs culled from the *Peterson's* guide, which charges a fee for listings, is far from comprehensive. Even though the voluminous program listings in *Peterson's* will make your eyes glaze over, many programs aren't included. Our program — the University of Dayton's London Communication program — wasn't.

By this point, all the program possibilities probably have you salivating so much that anyone who has been in the room with you for the past quarter hour fears that you have rabies and is backing carefully out the door. We will now sketch a few programs to give you a sense of the variety of program focuses and structures. We're sorry. We know this will only make your London yen worse. (If you just thought, *Wait a minute — isn't the British currency the pound?* you have disqualified yourself from London study. Close the book. Do not pass Go. Do not collect $200 . . . or £200 . . . or ¥200.)

The following programs are real, but we have cloaked their identities.

Program A: Blank State University

Blank State University has a spring-semester program called the London Centre Program. In a recent semester, students paid $1272 tuition plus a $6200 program fee, which covered airfare, housing, food, London transport, and a "cultural package" composed of special events such as plays, concerts, and walking tours, as well as day trips outside London. Students arrived in London January 8 and departed April 2.

Courses were taught by Blank State faculty and local experts. A variety of courses were offered, but the program had a media emphasis. Courses were:

ART HISTORY
BRITISH LIFE AND CULTURE
EUROPEAN HISTORY
THEATRE
MASS MEDIA IN SOCIETY
MASS MEDIA WRITING AND EDITING 2
MAGAZINE WRITING
JOURNALISM LAW
INTRODUCTION TO MASS MEDIA RESEARCH STRATEGIES
INDIVIDUAL STUDIES IN JOURNALISM.

Students registered for 12–15 credit hours.

A journalism professor from Blank State served as on-site director and taught the media courses. Another Blank State professor taught *European History*. *Art History* was taught by a senior lecturer from the Tate Gallery in London, and *Theatre* was taught by a professor from the City of Westminster College in London.

Blank State University's program was headquartered in a hotel.

Program B: The University of Somestate

The University of Somestate offers a semester program in London for honors students. The Honors Semester in London is offered in both the fall and spring term. A professor from the University of Somestate serves as the on-site program director, while other courses are typically taught by London academics.

Students take five or six three-credit classes, including a required course called *The London Experience*. Course offerings vary each term. To get a sense of the possibilities, let's take a closer look at the slate of courses during one recent semester:

BRITISH CINEMA AND BRITISH CULTURE SINCE WORLD WAR II
THE BRITISH MUSEUM, SOCIETY AND CULTURE: 1753–2000
LAWYERS, COURTS, AND THE LAW IN ENGLAND AND THE UNITED
  STATES: A COMPARATIVE INTRODUCTION
GLOBALIZATION OR MANAGEMENT AND BUSINESS
LONDON'S CONTEMPORARY POETS VERSUS YOUR OWN CREATIVE
  INSIGHTS
THE LONDON MUSIC SCENE — A CULTURAL HISTORY
SHAKESPEARE AND OTHER PLAYWRIGHTS IN PERFORMANCE
DISEASE AND THE SOCIAL ORDER: EUROPE AND THE UNITED STATES
  FROM 1700
CONTEMPORARY BRITISH POLITICS

Classes typically meet once a week for two to three hours over the 13-week program. Classes are held Tuesday through Friday, giving students three-day weekends to explore.

The University of Somestate program is located at the London Study Centre in the Bloomsbury section of London. Students are housed in furnished two- and three-bedroom apartments near the London Study Centre.

The program requires sophomore standing and is only open to students of the University of Somestate. The program requires a minimum grade-point average of 3.0 (a B average) and is limited to 30 students per term. Students paid, in a recent semester, $3248 tuition and general fees, plus a $2252 room fee, a $250 security deposit, and $86 for insurance. Airfare was not included, and students were responsible for their own meals.

Program C: Littletown College

Littletown College has a semester-abroad program, but it also has a three-week London program for the winter mini-term. The Winter Term in London, which has been taught annually for 30 years, offers students four credit hours.

When we checked, the three-week program, held January 5 to January 28, offered courses dealing with British media, literature, fine arts, history, and sociology, as well as a course on the British experience in the global marketplace. All six courses were taught by Littletown College faculty members.

The program cost of $2300 included airfare from New York, accommodations, breakfast, and ground transportation. Some admissions, activities, day trips, and course-related costs were also included. Tuition had been lumped in with the fall-semester bill.

The program was headquartered in the Bayswater area of London at two hotels located near each other. The program included a three-night stay in Edinburgh.

Just in case we described the perfect program for you and you want to follow up, or if your curiousity has you about to burst, we'll spill the goods. The first program described is offered by Ball State University, the second by the University of North Carolina, and the third by Elon College in North Carolina.

Why these three? They make perfectly good examples, and we have succumbed to human nature.

When you see a list like the *Peterson's* one we printed, the natural reaction is to skim it to see if your own college or one near your home appears. In fact, none of the universities that we attended appeared on the list, which prompted us to hurl ourselves into cyberspace and scout for more information. A quick World Wide Web search was enlightening. One of us is a Ball State alumnus, and the other is a University of North Carolina alumnus. Elon College is the nearest college to one of our hometowns.

Besides providing an excuse for a little plug for our own schools and hometown favorites, our World Wide Web search proved what a valuable tool the Web has become in ferreting out information pertaining to study abroad. You can use the Web to investigate your own school's programs or those of a school halfway across the country. You can check any time of the day or night. You can launch a broad search — let's say, for example, into London programs for theatre students — or you can search with pinpoint precision. And depending on how you get your Web access, it may be completely free! So spend a few hours casting your net on the Internet (sorry . . . couldn't resist).

Here's an example of a London study opportunity that's much more specialized than the ones described above. The London Academy of Performing Arts, located in the Fulham area, is a classic drama school aimed at training theatre actors. The academy offers a range of programs. A four-week program offered in July and August focuses on Shakespearean acting. The Classical Acting Semester, a 12–week program offered from September to December, is aimed at university students, particularly those doing a semester abroad. The academy also has a two-year diploma in classical acting, with an optional concentration in musical theatre. Year-long post-graduate programs focus on classical acting, musical theatre, stage directing, and stage management.

A particularly good Web site for pondering the myriad possibilities is *http://www.studyabroad.com*. This site offers helpful tips and lists many program options. You can even search for a program by subject matter. Some programs here weren't in the *Peterson's* guide, but these listings aren't all-inclusive either. It's unlikely that any guide, traditionally published and constrained by costs and size, or Internet-based and thus theoretically unlimited in scope, will ever contain all the possibilities. There are simply too many, and they change from year to year.

Which brings us back to the point that the best place to start is the study-abroad/international-educational program office at your college. You can save time that way and get information that often goes beyond what is publicly available. The international-program advisor can describe not only your school's options but can also tell you how students from your college fared when going on programs through other schools or organizations.  Let's say, hypothetically, that you are considering studying through the American College in London. The international-program advisor may be able to provide insight into various academic and social elements of American College in London. Maybe she has brochures from American College in London. Maybe two students from your college enrolled last semester, and the advisor can relate their level of satisfaction with the experience. She may give you their phone numbers so that you can ask them questions yourself. The advisor can also guide you through the enrollment process and let you know how the credits and grades will transfer.

The bottom line — do your homework by considering your options carefully. Ask a lot of questions. Choose the program that is right for you. But *do* choose a program — because studying in London will be one of the most rewarding things you ever do.

As long as we're on the subject of making wise choices, after you've settled on a program, you'll want to give some thought to what courses you'll take in the program. The most appropriate courses for study abroad, no matter the site, are those for which the material can be readily and closely linked to the site. The closer the link, the better. Thus, *20th-Century British Literature* is a more appropriate offering than *20th-Century European Literature*, which is, in turn, more appropriate than *20th-Century World Literature.* Much depends on the professor. The *20th-Century European Literature* class could be approached in a way that emphasizes British writers.

College committees may (and many do) debate *ad infinitum* what sorts of courses to offer in a study-abroad program. The course offerings may reflect concerns other than merely assembling a roster of the most appropriate courses for the site. They may be driven by enrollment concerns, so course offerings may include classes that are required for all students or those historically popular on campus and thus likely to attract students for the abroad program as well. The choice of course offerings may also reflect the self-serving idea that study-abroad programs should be designed so that every professor can teach abroad, regardless of the appropriateness of the course. So it is important for you to put considerable thought into what courses you enroll in for your London study.

Reflect on your goals. Are you trying to fulfill particular requirements for your major or general college requirements? Perhaps you don't need the classes for any particular requirements and are simply interested in good courses that relate well to London.

Assuming that you have a choice, consider what material would be the most exciting and useful to study in London. If you choose your courses before you arrive, ask the professors or program administrators for any tentative syllabi or course outlines they might have. Find out what special activities are planned or in the works. Find out what sort of readings there are. Of course, this would be sound advice for a course you take on campus as well, but this aggressive approach really pays off for your study-abroad courses. You owe it to yourself to choose courses that you are interested in.

London Study Before College

Many high schools offer European trips of short duration, but the vast majority aren't really academically oriented. A high school student wanting to study in London might be best served by going through an organization that focuses on international-educational opportunities or by enrolling directly at a British institution offering such study. The same advice we offered earlier to college students applies here: go to your school's guidance counselor for suggestions.

We will describe a few opportunities for London study for pre-college students.

Many high school students go abroad through an academic exchange. One such organization that can arrange exchanges of different durations in locations throughout England is AYUSA International, which is based in San Francisco. AYUSA students live with a host family while abroad.

AYUSA exchange students must be 15 to 18 years old and must have at least a 2.75 grade-point average for an academic-year exchange and a 2.5 for a summer exchange.

You may opt to study directly through a school in London or thereabouts. The TASIS England American School, located six miles from Heathrow Airport in the village of Thorpe, just southeast of London, offers a special summer program for students 12 to 18 years old. Students from all over the world enroll in the program, in which they take classes in a range of subjects from 9 A.M. to 2 P.M. Afternoons are devoted to sports, while the school organizes weekend travel and cultural opportunities. TASIS also offers an academic-year program for students aged 4 to 18.

Another example of a school with both a year-round program and a special summer program is the Southbank International School, whose students range from 3 to 18. This school has two London campuses — one in the Notting Hill Gate area and another in Hampstead. The original site of the school was on the South Bank of the Thames, but the school retained the name after relocating.

The promotional literature of the Southbank International School contains the magic phrase that you look for in choosing a program, no matter what institution is offering it: *London itself — its people, museums, theatres, and civic institutions — is used as an extension of the campus and the curriculum.* What's magic about the phrase? It contains the educational philosophy that you are looking for in any London program. This premise should underlie every aspect of a London program because the whole point of studying abroad is to take advantage of the opportunities for educational and cultural enrichment. In building our university department's London program, we have constantly upheld the same idea.

Chapter 4

How Do I Fund This Little Academic Adventure?

The biggest concern we see about foreign study, in student after student, year after year, is not the idea of traveling to another country, not the idea of being away from home and friends for weeks or months, not concerns about safety in other parts of the world, not even the idea of missing the tasty meals served in the school cafeteria. The biggest continuing worry is *How do I pay for it?*

We have arguments to counter any objection a student raises to foreign study except *I really can't afford it*. But we know that frequently students *can* afford it — they just haven't realized all the possibilities.

First of all, let's acknowledge that not many of us have as much money as we'd like. We have to make choices about how to spend what we *do* have. *I've only* *got $10 left. Do I buy a birthday present for my sister, get that copy of Plato I need for my philosophy class, or go out with my friends tonight?* Based solely on personal experience, we're betting you send sis a card, get Plato from the library, and party on tonight!

The point is this: you make choices. You establish priorities. If we've been successful so far in persuading you that studying in London is something you want to do, the first step in *affording* to do it is to decide to pursue it! Once you make that decision and make the trip a priority, you can begin to see what trade-offs are available to allow you to go abroad.

Get rid of the notion that *after I graduate, I'll have more money and I can go abroad then.* Maybe that will happen, but more likely it won't. After graduation your responsibilities usually increase dramatically — and you may have less money than you do now. For most people, graduation means a job, a regular paycheck that is a lot bigger than the one you get working for Food Service now. But it also means more expenses: rent . . . car payments . . . car and health and life insurance . . . payback of student loans . . . new clothes, suitable for work . . . the list is endless.

A whole new level of responsibility comes with graduation, too. A regular job with limited vacation time. Marriage? Family? Down payment on a house?

Frankly, if you don't travel abroad as a student, you may find it to be a long time before you get the chance again. You may feel busy and broke now but wait a couple of years: you're sure to be either busier or more broke. We just hope it's not both.

Besides, traveling abroad saves you money in unexpected ways when you're a student. Let's look at some.

Tuition: If you're careful about choosing a program and the courses you take, the credits you earn will count toward graduation. If an English major takes six semester hours of English classes in London one summer, that should be six hours less that he has to take (and pay for!) on campus.

It gets better. A student in *any* major has to take some kind of General Education or Core Area classes at almost every university. You know what we mean: two history classes, two philosophy classes, two science classes, etc. If a student can take in London four or five classes that will count toward this Gen Ed requirement, she might be able to graduate a semester early — saving a semester's worth of tuition. That means if you pay $5000 for a summer in London and it nets you a semester's worth of credits, and you save $3000 in tuition by graduating a semester early, the London program really cost you only $2000. What a bargain!

The same thing is true of high school students, although except for private or parochial school students, tuition costs may not be an issue. Early graduation or advanced placement in higher-level courses is possible if you can apply to your requirements at home the credits you earn abroad.

It's important that you talk to your advisor, department chairperson, dean, or guidance counselor about this before you go. That is the person who will decide what counts toward graduation and what doesn't. But chances are that person will recognize the tremendous benefits of studying abroad and will be eager to help you arrange your schedule to take advantage of the opportunity.

Employment at Home: Your trip will cost money — there's no getting around it. But unless you're already stretched to the limit, you ought to be able to earn at least enough extra money to pay for a summer program. You can find summer programs that last from two to six weeks and schedules that still allow you to work during much of the summer — perhaps almost as much as you usually do anyway.

If you sign up for a summer program that falls in the middle of the summer, as many do, don't lose heart. We have actually seen few employers who won't let you work both before and after your trip, provided you agree to bring them back a pint of good English ale or a keychain with a picture of the Queen Mum on it. Tell your boss what a good, once-in-a-lifetime opportunity this is for you and chances are very good he'll go along with the plan.

Formal internship programs are a little more difficult to skip, since they are often tightly structured. If you can't take your internship during the school year, you may have to choose between interning and studying abroad — unless you can find an *internship* abroad. More about that in a minute.

Many students also pick up a week or two of work when they go home for Christmas, intersession, or spring holidays, then put the money in their London Fund. Is that as much fun as spending your vacation loafing? Of course not! But the payoff comes next summer as you window-shop your way down Piccadilly.

If you don't have a job at school already, getting one can pay most of your way. A 15-hour-per-week job at $5.50 per hour this year will pay for half of what a five- or six-week program in London will cost next summer. Not a single one of the many, many students we've seen do this has said it wasn't worth it. We've also known students who have picked up an extra part-time job in addition to their full-time summer job the year before they planned to go abroad. The agonies of your summer of hard work are *always* replaced in your memory by your summer of gazing at Big Ben and the Thames.

Employment in London: We've known students who have gone to London both to study *and* work. Working is not always easy, and it can cut into the free time you have to see the sights, but it's an unparalleled way to meet people and see a different side of life from what most students see. And it helps with expenses.

Finding part-time work in London isn't hard, but it takes careful planning because you have to get permission in advance. You are not allowed to work when you enter Britain in the normal way as a student or tourist. In fact, your passport, if you're not a citizen of a country in the European Union, will probably be stamped *Leave to enter for 6 months. Employment prohibited.*

If employment is an option that interests you, students from the United States and Canada should contact the British Universities North America Club (BUNAC) for information about obtaining a Blue Card that allows students to work for six months in Britain. The address is:

BUNAC USA
PO Box 49
New Britain, CT 06487 USA
(203) 264-0901

From June 15 to October 4
the telephone number for BUNAC is (212) 316-5312

Students from other countries should contact the nearest British consulate for information about how to obtain temporary work permits.

Another outstanding source for overseas work is the Council on International Educational Exchange (CIEE), often just referred to as "Council." CIEE runs its own travel agency, Council Travel, which offers some of the lowest possible airline rates and extensive information about studying and working abroad. Council Travel has several offices in the United States, one in London, five in France, two in Germany, and one each in Japan, Singapore, and Thailand. CIEE can be reached at:

CIEE: Council on International Educational Exchange
205 E. 42nd Street
New York, NY 10017-5706 USA

or through its Web page at *http://www.ciee.org*

Typical short-term jobs for students include work in pubs and restaurants, hotels, and retail shops. The pay probably won't be greatly different from what you'd receive for a comparable job at home, but it will be enough to pay your day-to-day expenses once you're there. Look for a job in London the same way you would at home. Apply to places you think you'd like to work. There are other avenues, too. The local pub keeper knows most of what's going on in the neighborhood. Ask him if he knows of anyone who would like to hire some short-term help. Also, look for the local neighborhood center. Many have message boards outside that include job postings for the sort of thing you're probably seeking. There are also local newspapers that may have some listings. Tip: the free weekly paper *Loot* is available on the World Wide Web at *http://www.lootlink.com* and includes part-time jobs. If you're associated with the BUNAC or CIEE programs, they can help you find work.

Internships in London: We've had students, too, who have combined the advantages of foreign study with the advantages of doing an internship, something that *really* causes prospective employers to sit up and take notice. As you investigate internship opportunities with any large international corporation, ask about the possibility of obtaining an internship in its London office. Opportunities are not uncommon in print and broadcasting, business and advertising, and other fields, and you, as a foreign intern, may be even more exotic and desirable than a native. Look especially for London offices of companies that are based in your home country.

You will probably have to go through the international employment approval process we described above, and your stay in Britain may still be limited to a fixed time, like six months, but when you return home you'll have had a truly unique — and very rewarding — experience.

Financial Aid: Financial aid is a complicated area because there are so many different types of aid programs that may vary dizzyingly from state to state and country to country. Your best bet is to see the person who coordinates your financial arrangements at your home school. In the United States, students who are eligible for financial aid during the regular academic year are normally eligible for aid for a foreign-study program. But conditions vary wildly. There might be a maximum amount per year, which you can apply to classes you take anywhere. There might be limitations on the types of schools or programs at which you can receive aid. You may not be eligible for financial aid if you are enrolled in a program sponsored by a university other than your own. On the other hand, if you've been successful in landing an *internship* in London, chances are that your financial aid will apply as long as you are doing the work for credit. Only your financial-aid counselor can tell you exactly how each situation will pertain to your own particular circumstances. Begin checking out financial-aid opportunities early, avoiding the beginning- and end-of-term rush in that office. You want to keep the financial-aid people on your side, and the best way to do that is when there's not a line of people 17 deep at the desk, all clamoring for money.

Living Frugally: London can be one of the most expensive cities in the world. However, since you won't be traveling on an expense account and since very few financial-aid packages or part-time jobs pay enough for you to bunk at the Dorchester, you'll have to watch your expenses. That's not really difficult at all. London is, after all, a city of more than seven million people. Most Londoners are just normal, ordinary garden-variety people, no better off financially than you are. They manage quite nicely, if not lavishly. So can you.

Housing: Lodging may very well be a part of the London program you participate in. If it's during the summer, chances are you'll stay in a student residence hall or apartment complex at the University of London, Imperial College, Richmond College, or somewhere comparable. This is convenient because it gives you one less thing to worry about. Breakfast and certain other meals probably will be included, or else you'll have cooking facilities in your lodgings.

If you are expected to find your own digs, don't panic. Short-term housing is plentiful in London and can be very economical. If you're making any of your arrangements through BUNAC or Council Travel, they can help you find a convenient and inexpensive place to stay. BUNAC suggests that students wait until they arrive before looking for a place to live. Both groups will put you up in a hostel for a few days while you get your bearings, and both have extensive listings for inexpensive lodgings.

Food: Take advantage of all the meals your study program provides, usually a big breakfast daily, at the least. For other meals, though, there are three good possibilities:

One: If you have cooking facilities, the cheapest route is to fix many meals yourself. You can get everything you need from the corner markets you'll find in every neighborhood. There's usually a big Tesco or Sainsbury's close by, too. Be sure to shop at the local produce markets you'll find everywhere for inexpensive fruits and vegetables.

Two: Hard as it is for most students to believe, there's more to most pubs than the beer! Most pubs serve inexpensive lunches and many serve evening meals, too. These meals are always a good value and often include traditional English favorites like meat pies or bangers and mash — sausages and mashed potatoes.

Three: Think ethnic. If you haven't eaten Indian food, you're in for a real treat. Indian restaurants abound, as do Chinese, Greek, and Middle Eastern — all at prices much less than what you'd pay for more familiar fare. Be adventurous! If all you wanted was the same old thing, you could have stayed home.

Transportation: London has one of the world's best networks of city transportation. Using its famous Underground, lumbering red double-decker buses, and ubiquitous black taxis, people get though the chaos and mayhem of city crowds with amazing efficiency (unless one or another of the drivers' unions is on strike). As we explain in Chapter 6, your best bet is to buy a London Transport pass. Even taxis are fairly inexpensive, since London is so compact. But the best way of getting around is to walk. You can walk from one end of the city to the other in a couple of hours, discovering delightful and amusing things all along the way, not to mention passing (or *not* passing, perhaps) dozens of interesting and historic pubs along your route.

We've always admitted to students interested in our programs that, yes, going to London can cost a lot of money. There are creative ways to minimize the cost, but honestly, it's worth twice the price! You'll spend the money on something anyway, and money is something you can always earn more of later. Missing your opportunity to study in one of the world's most exciting cities, though, may be something that you just *can't* get back, not ever. If you miss your chance now, the opportunity may not come again for years.

Chapter 5

I'm Convinced! How Do I Get Ready?

The challenge for this chapter is not merely to lead you to sources of information about London, it's to help you make sense of the incredible amount of stuff out there! Within three feet of the shelf you took this book from, there were probably 30 other books about London. If you could afford all those books, you could just move there for awhile — heck with studying!

All those books are just the tip of the literary iceberg. There is no way you can survey all the books, look at all the Web sites, write for all the brochures, or make all the lists you need to get ready for your trip. Because London is one of the most popular travel destinations in the world, more new material becomes available each week than we could possibly catalog.

That doesn't mean you should turn up at Heathrow without a shred of advance planning. If you choose that route, we can direct you to a rather extensive cardboard-box city not far from Waterloo Station. But perhaps you shouldn't give that address to your mother.

Actually, we've always felt that the excitement of planning for a trip is the next best thing to actually being there. When we teach there in the summer, we start our planning the previous autumn — not because we *need* to. We've made this trip so often that London's practically a home away from home by now. But the anticipation — deciding what new things we'll see and what old favorites we'll return to, thinking with pleasure about seeing the friends we have over there, reading the theatre listings to see what might be playing while we're in town — those are the things that fill our winter evenings.

We read new books about London (and sometimes write them), cruise the Web, chat with Internet acquaintances about their trips, make lists and plans — all to get ready to return to a place we already know well. There's just one reason for it: it's part of the fun.

Savor the planning. It allows you to take the trip three times — first while you're getting ready to go, again while you're actually there, and finally through all your memories, photographs, and journals once you're home again. Take away the planning, and it takes longer to become part of your new surroundings and much longer to make connections among all the new things you see and do. Reading this book is the start of an exciting process for you.

This won't be the only guidebook you read,

though. You ought to look through one or two others that provide a more general overview of the city, ones that spend more time than we do with the traditional tourist sights. You'll be seeing a lot of pretty cool new things, and they will make more sense to you if you've read a bit about them. Your library will have several standard guidebooks you can borrow.

General Information: Guidebooks, however, may not be the most up-to-date sources of information. (This one is the exception, of course! Obviously there's no better source of information than this book. We asked our own students and they said, yes, they were forced to agree . . . .) Specialized books about something of particular interest to you are tremendously helpful. But a book's information gets frozen in time once it's printed. At least that used to be the case. We *are* able to keep this book current by posting updates on the World Wide Web on our page at:

http://www.as.udayton.edu/com/faculty/student.htm

You can also use the Web effectively to gather the latest general information about London as well as much specific information. Below is a list of other Web sites we think will be helpful to you in making plans and a few words about why we recommend them.

Yahoo UK: Yahoo always has an outstanding collection of links, but most people don't know they have a Web site dedicated just to the United Kingdom and Ireland. This site can lead you to just about everything you might ever want to know except where to get a date on Friday night, although maybe if you check out

the Entertainment or Recreation sections . . . .
(http://www.yahoo.co.uk/)

Dr. Dave's UK Pages: Here is a nice suite of original information and links offering a wide array of pages from academics to tourism. This American Anglophile's page can help you find a place to stay in London and show you what to do when you get there. *(http://www.neosoft.com/ ~ dlgates/uk/ukgeneral.html)*

British Tourist Authority: The BTA has completely revamped its original site into a huge suite of pages covering all of Great Britain. Emphasis here is on tourism, but the site is rich in practical information — from using the telephone system to finding a short-term job to learning English. *(http://www.visitbritain.com/)*

City University's Guide: This is a less extensive site than the previous three, but it provides student perspectives on where to go and what to do in London. It's a good chance to see where British students hang out. *(http://web.cs.city.ac.uk/london/guide.html)*

London Tourist Board: This is an easy-to-use site that not only outlines the usual attractions, but offers information that is hard to find in other places. Here you can scope out tours of plants and businesses that pertain to your area of study, local colleges, and much more. *(http://www.LondonTown.com)*

Travelling in the UK: A London college professor maintains this page. It's visually uninteresting, but rich in good practical information on travel and transportation. *(http://www.city.ac.uk/martin/ukfaq.html)*

London Transport: This source gives you absolutely everything you could want to know about the

Tube and buses.
(http://www.londontransport.co.uk/)

   British Rail: The guide to trains in the United Kingdom. Note that the British *never* call it "Britrail." That's just for tourists and the BR marketing department. *(http://www.britrail.com)*

   There are scores, perhaps hundreds of other Web links, but these are the ones we use most. If you can't find it here, you probably don't need to know it. (And yes, there *is* a Web site that can help you get a date on Friday night, but we don't use it — our wives wouldn't be pleased.)

   You can also write for information in the more conventional way. Before you go abroad, you can get stacks of information from the British Tourist Authority (BTA). BTA can provide an excellent map of London that's free — unless you wait until you get there. Then it will cost you £1.50. The tourist agency will also send you a heavy envelope full of goodies. BTA has offices in 26 countries. For a complete list of addresses and telephone numbers, write to the BTA at:

British Tourist Authority
Thames Tower
Black's Road
London W6 9EL United Kingdom

   If you're lucky enough to live near one of their locations, visit the BTA office. We carry away 10 or 20 *pounds* of booklets, pamphlets, brochures, and maps every time we're in New York or Chicago. That's "pounds" as in weight, not money — nearly all the

material is free for the taking. The only limit is the strength of your back.

The London Tourist Board will happily send you material, too. If you have to find your own place to stay while you're studying in London, ask for their booklets *Accommodations for Budget Travellers* and *Where to Stay in London*. Both booklets are filled with listings and descriptions of places where you can afford to live. Write them at:

London Tourist Board
26 Grosvenor Gardens
London SW1W 0DU United Kingdom

Controlling Costs: You will have three major categories of expenses on your study trip. The first, *the cost of the study program itself*, you have little or no control over except, perhaps, in deciding how many classes to take. But then you pay the going rate; few schools will negotiate the price with you. If lodging and meals are included, as is often the case, they are chargeable at a fixed rate. The only effective way you can control program costs is through the program you choose to go on.

For many students, the next big cost will be *getting to London*. If you're just coming over from Italy or Spain, this is a minor expense. But students from the Americas, Asia, and Oceania may find the airfare daunting. There are some tricks you need to know to get good airfares, however. We believe, too, that you are usually better off using the services of a travel agent with extensive international experience. This person can find you the best fares much more quickly and effectively than you can, even if you feel perfectly comfortable booking your own flights through the Internet. Not every special fare is posted there.

Your travel agent can check not only scheduled airlines but also consolidators — companies that buy large blocks of discounted tickets on scheduled airlines and then sell them for less than the airlines themselves do. Your agent will know which companies are trustworthy.

Flexibility is the key to getting the best fare. You can save money on travel, and perhaps on lodging, if you go on a program that does not correspond to summer in the Northern Hemisphere. Summer is "high season" for airlines, and fares are 30 to 50 percent or more higher at this time. But your choice of programs probably will not be dictated by trying to save a few hundred dollars on airfare, so let's look at a few other ways to save a sou or two.

- **Don't fly on weekends.** Fares are higher if you fly on Friday, Saturday, or Sunday. If you have to be in London Saturday, it may well be cheaper to fly Thursday and pay an extra night's lodging than to fly on Friday.
- **Shop around for different airports.** Fares from your hometown airport may not be the best. Check prices from any airport you can get to easily; an hour's drive could save you more than $100.
- **Consider connecting flights.** Non-stop flights are usually the most expensive, because people are willing to pay for convenience. You can often get a real bargain if you're willing to change planes once or twice.
- **Shop all the airlines.** Don't just stick to your own major national carriers. Bargains can often be had on the national airlines of *other* countries. One friend flew from New York to London on the first leg of an Air India flight from New York to New Delhi and saved hundreds of dollars.
- **Watch for sales.** The airline business is highly competitive in many countries, and bargain fares come and go without warning. Be

ready to leap on a good fare. If a sale comes along *after* you've purchased a ticket, many airlines will reduce your fare to the sale rate but *only if you ask.* You might have to pay a service fee for this.

CIEE (Council) has a student travel agency with excellent fares. If you live near one of the CIEE gateway cities, it's worth checking to see if they can beat the rate available to your local travel agent. They often can.

Council Travel or your own travel agent can also sell you a Britrail train pass if you plan to do much out-of-London sightseeing. Britrail passes are available for one or two months and allow unlimited travel on virtually all trains. A better bet is the Britrail Flexipass. These passes are good for any 4, 8, or 15 days in a month, depending on how much you plan to travel. And since you're going over there to *study,* you're not likely to be traveling every day. A month in Britain will surely be enriched by a couple of weekend trips and some afternoon day trips, so for most people, an eight-day pass is enough.

Don't waste money on a first-class rail pass. It's a lot more expensive and not that much more comfortable. British Rail's standard-class service isn't anything like "hard class" in some parts of the world. All intercity carriages are air conditioned and comfortable, and journeys are short. London to Edinburgh, for example, is just four hours. And the entire train gets to its destination at the same time — it's not like second class takes an extra half-hour or anything! And you're unlikely to meet the Queen, even in first class.

Discounts on rail passes are available for students, so be sure to ask for them. And here's something important:

Buy your rail pass before you leave home. Passes are *not* available inside Britain.

If you don't plan to travel enough to make a rail pass worthwhile, intercity train travel can still be inexpensive. If you plan your long weekend to the Scottish Highlands well in advance, you can get supersaver APEX fares at a discount, just as you can with airline tickets. These are much cheaper than standard rates. If you're just popping up to Oxford for an afternoon, ask for a "cheap day return" ticket, also much less expensive than an open ticket.

The third major expense you face is *shopping*. Our students always ask us how much shopping money they ought to take, and that's a question we just can't answer. It's much easier to give advice about other expenses, like food. (In fact, if you were paying attention, you'll recall that we did that in the last chapter.) We've literally seen students go home from London a thousand pounds lighter after just a month of determined souvenir shopping. (We mean money this time, not weight. All our students have had hearty appetites.) A few determined shoppers have had to buy extra luggage to carry all their loot. That's crazy!

Set a souvenir and gift budget and stick to it. That's not hard to do if you avoid shopping in tourist areas and big shopping meccas such as South Kensington and Oxford Street. There are plenty of neighborhood shopping streets and complexes in the places visitors never go. Besides, the best souvenirs will be your photos and journal. We don't think you should spend much more when you go to school in London than you do at home. If you *must* make a major purchase, though, use your credit card, not cash. You'll save money on the exchange rate, and you won't deplete your cash reserves.

Packing: Everybody overpacks. Once. The best time to get overpacking out of your system is to do it before you leave. Pack everything you want to take. Cram your suitcases full of stuff you might need "just in case." Then pick up those bags and carry them around the block. All the way around. No cheating. Got that out of your system? That's how you *want* to pack, and it wasn't very much fun, we bet. Now let's look at how you *should* pack.

First of all, limit yourself to *one* checked bag and *one* carry-on, even if you're allowed more.

Your authors disagree slightly on this point. Jeff never checks a bag but takes everything he needs for five weeks or more in a carry-on. He never has to worry about waiting for luggage to come off the plane, and the airlines never have a chance to lose it.

Larry acknowledges that but still thinks it's crazy

and compulsive for a trip of a month or more. Besides, he's bigger than Jeff and his clothes take up more room. He'll allow you one checked bag. Take your choice.

Planning to do a little laundry every few days, even if it's just washing out underwear and socks and hanging them to dry in your room, means that you don't need to take weeks' worth of clothing. Below is a list of what we think you should pack. Sometimes we give a range, depending on how long you plan to stay. Remember that you're wearing clothes, too! If you're planning to check a bag, you still need to take a carry-on; items in the following list that should be in your carry-on are marked with an asterisk (*).

Clothing: Two or three pairs of slacks and/or skirts; three to six shirts or blouses; several days' worth of underwear; six to eight pairs of socks or hose; handkerchiefs; sleepwear; at least one extra pair of shoes; sweater; seasonal outerwear; one dressier outfit.

Other gear: Guidebook; map of London; camera and film*; alarm clock; sunglasses; a small radio (remove the batteries!); your journal*; medicines and prescriptions*; umbrella; string bag or laundry bag; inflatable pillow; small towel; book to read on the plane*.

Also consider packing a snack* in case your plane is late and dinner is delayed (this happens to Larry all the time). If you're checking a bag, make sure you have some clean clothes in your carry-on, just in case Jeff's right and your luggage takes a different route to London than you do. Don't bother with electrical equipment you can manage without. Hair driers and such things from North America and some other places will require power converters that may cost more than an inexpensive hair drier in London.

Two things should *never, never, never* be in your checked luggage — your passport and your money. The best place for both is on your person. There is nothing in this book that we urge more strongly than the purchase of a money belt or neck pouch. It is essential to your financial security and your peace of mind.

A money belt is worn around your waist under your trousers, and a neck pouch goes inside your shirt. Whichever you find more comfortable (one of your authors wears a money belt, the other a neck pouch), it is absolutely the only place for your cash, except for what you expect to spend each day; it's the safest place for your passport, too. Violent crime is unusual in London, but pickpocketry is not. A simple $10 purchase can save you hundreds of pounds of worry.

Carrying Your Money: That leads us to the pivotal question: *How much money should I take?* We don't know. We don't know what expenses your program covers, we don't know your shopping habits, we don't know anything about you except that you are a highly intelligent person. (Why else would you have had the good sense to buy our book?) As a guideline, though, look at what you would spend for food, entertainment, and shopping for a comparable period *on campus*. Add about 25 percent to that and you'll probably come close. You'll spend more per day, on the average, for a short stay than for a long one, so if you're on a two- or three-week program, you might add extra money. If you're there for six months, 10 or 15 percent might do.

Experts debate how it's best to carry money — dollars (or yen, francs, or pesos) or pounds, cash, traveler's cheques, or credit cards — and there's no easy answer. If you convert your own currency to pounds before the trip, you have the advantage of being ready to go when you step off the plane and that's what we usually do. Most of our money is in traveler's cheques in pound denominations, with enough cash for a day or two. It's becoming more economical, however, to get cash from ATMs — bank machines, often called Cash Points in London. The exchange rate is probably the best you're likely to get, because charges are based on the commercial rate, not the higher consumer rate.

Your bank card needs a four-digit PIN number (not a word). You'll find cash machines all over London. But don't wait until you're out of money before seeking one out. Sometimes they're behind locked doors on weekends, and only bank customers can get in to use them.

Planning for a trip of this scope can be a lot of work, but it's fun to do and will just heighten the excitement of the experience. Planning, thinking about, and getting ready for your adventure is one of the great joys of travel. We truly look forward to going, but we look forward to the preliminaries, too. It's like spending the day smelling the big Christmas dinner in the oven. By the time supper is on the table, your juices are really flowing. You're ready for dinner!

So it is with travel.

Chapter 6

OK, I've Arrived. So What Do I Do Next?

Your plane has just landed, probably at Heathrow or Gatwick, the two major airports serving London. If your carrier was Frank's Discount Airline and Crop Spraying, you might have flown into a third airport, Stanstead.

Getting into London from Heathrow or Gatwick is a snap. From Heathrow, you can take the Piccadilly Line of the Underground (also known as "the Tube"), the Airbus service into Central London, or the new high-speed rail link to Paddington Station. From Gatwick, there's the Gatwick Express train to Victoria Station in Central London. Once you are in the heart of London, the simplest way to get to your lodging is to take a licensed taxi, likely one of those old-fashioned black sedans that become etched in visitors' mental images of London in the same way that red double-decker buses and "bobbies" in their distinctive headgear do.

Of course, you may not have flown at all. Perhaps you've arrived in England footsore and wearing clothes in desperate need of laundering after three weeks of backpacking through the continent. If so, you've probably taken the Chunnel train to Waterloo Station or disembarked from the ferry at Dover and taken a train into London. It doesn't matter. What's important is that you're here.

Once you've ditched your gear at the hotel, residence hall, or whatever place you will call home, you may be able to hit the streets for some preliminary reconnaissance before you succumb to jet lag. The exhilaration of finding yourself in London probably gives you enough adrenaline to have a look-see and a bite to eat. Don't get cocky — unless you've come over from the Continent, jet lag *will* lay waste to your energy — it's just a question of when. You might even pay homage to that great British institution, the pub, by stopping in one for a half-pint or pint of ale, an overpriced cola, or a Perrier and a chance to reflect on the wonderful adventure that you are beginning. This is the perfect time to start a journal.

Notice that we use the word *journal* instead of diary. *Journals* are for travelers. We will say or do just about anything to get you to write about what you see and experience in London. Jotting down your thoughts and recounting your adventures is a wonderful way to distill what is happening to you. Beyond that, the record of your trip will become, along with any photographs, slides, or videos you shoot, a treasured memory of your time in London. That pewter Tower Bridge will one day be banished to a box in the attic. The T-shirt from the Hard Rock Cafe will fall victim to an expanding waistline or a hungry moth. The group-of-the-moment CD that you bought at the massive Virgin music store on Oxford Street will become *passe*. The journal, however, is like a cryogenically frozen slice of your mind that can be reheated in the memory microwave anytime you want to journey back to London from your recliner. Unlike the other things you bring home, the journal's connectedness to you is permanent — in fact, the journal may survive a lot longer than do you! People today can get insight into the lives of Londoners in centuries past by reading the journals of such residents as Samuel Pepys (1633–1703). Pepys, who eventually became secretary of the admiralty, witnessed the Great Fire of London in 1666 after having survived the plague the previous year. We hope your time will be equally momentous but loads more fun.

To be forthright, keeping a journal has a downside — in fact, it's a minor pain in your downside. The problem is TIME . . . you don't have nearly *enough time*, and you are going at full speed *all the time*, so to *find the time* to make your journal entries isn't easy. You will inevitably fall behind, and remembering what you ate for lunch last Thursday or the name of that good-looking fellow traveler that you met Saturday night at the club in Edinburgh will drive you up the wall. Was that a Monet painting that so entranced you at the National Gallery or a Renoir? When it happens, don't be dismayed. Falling behind is an important part of the journal-keeping experience. If you are so well organized that you find time every single day to write 3½ pages in your journal before bedtime, then your anal-retentiveness dooms you to a humdrum life. Sometimes you don't have a half-hour to write in your journal because you are actually having such a terrific time that you can't afford to give up even a half-hour to record your day. Fine . . . that's as it should be. No one approach works for everyone.

Some people carry their journals around with them and use those odd snatches of 15 minutes here or there to put down some thoughts and record events. Others save up for those long stretches when there's little to distract them — for example, while on the train to York or Canterbury or while doing laundry. Write in your journal when you want to and in whatever form appeals to you. You may make note of even the smallest details — whether you had cereal and toast for breakfast or beans and bacon — and the things that moved you, such as a description of the stained-glass window in Westminster Abbey that rendered you speechless as the late afternoon sun angled through the bits of colored glass. You can write in it systematically or sporadically. How and when don't matter, but doing it does. You'll return to that journal time and again in the years to come, and it not only opens the floodgates of your memory, but it also gives you pause to think about who you *were*. At 20, it is easier to see *self* as a constant than it is at 40.

If pen and paper aren't your style, consider an

alternative approach. You might use a notebook computer. You might use a microcassette recorder to make an oral and aural record of your journey. Just tote the recorder around with you and speak into it when you have an observation or want to remember a moment. Record the church bells whose tones you find so mellifluous. Capture the sounds of traffic at Trafalgar Square or the roar of soccer fans at Wembley Stadium.

So, where were we? You've scouted the neighborhood, locating the nearest post office, pub, grocer, cheap eatery, and Tube station. You've firmly planted your flag in English soil, so to speak. Now you should get some sleep. A good strategy is to take a nap of two to three hours. No less, no more. The nap of two to three hours is really the perfect antidote to jet lag. Your body will virtually shut down the moment your head hits the pillow, so set an alarm. Once the chirping of your alarm has penetrated your near-coma, you will awake rather refreshed, though perhaps a bit loopy. But you'll feel good enough for an evening on the town. The best part is that the nap helped reset your body clock to Greenwich Mean Time. You will sleep the sleep-of-the-just later that night. The next morning, when some of you will have class, you will awake feeling like a million dollars (make that a million *pounds*). If you ignore the Nap Mandate or bend its rules, you will pay a price. With no nap or one too short, you'll keel over into your plate at dinner. With too long a nap, you'll not be able to sleep that night or you'll awaken at three in the morning. Trust us. We have loads of experience in trans-Atlantic body-clock resetting.

Once you've experienced your first English sunrise, it's time to get to know the city better. If you're taking part in a formal program operated by your university or some other entity, your program should include some orientation to London. That may involve class sessions, walking tours, a highlights-of-London bus tour, or all three. If your program doesn't adequately introduce you to the city, or if you arrived early to give yourself a chance to enjoy the city before your program starts, then you can figure things out on your own.

One important bit of advice is to buy the London Transport TravelCard, a metro pass that will enable you to use the Underground and city buses as much as you want without paying separately for each ride. The pass, which you should be able to buy at any Underground station, comes in a variety of durations and scopes. If you're going to be in London for awhile, a month-long pass is likely what you will need. The pass is good for all travel within certain zones. If you are going to be staying in some area of Central London, such as Bloomsbury or South Kensington, then you will likely need just a Zone 1 pass. On those occasions when you venture to outlying areas of London, you can buy a supplemental ticket to augment your pass. The pass is pricey — a month-long Zone 1 pass costs about £50 — but is much cheaper than paying each time you use a bus or the Underground. Convenience is another plus. If in doubt about your needs, consult the ticket seller and keep your fingers crossed that the person behind the glass is considerate rather than grumpy. For some reason, people who work in transportation ticket booths the world over seem to have the personality of the permanently constipated and regard foreigners with resignation or irritation more often than not. Anyway, to have a pass made, besides a wad of pound notes or a traveler's cheque in pounds sterling, you'll need a passport-size photo. Many Underground stations have little photo booths, so if you've forgotten to bring a head-and-shoulders shot to London, you can duck into one of these booths, look dignified for one shot and then make strange faces or bare your tattoo for the other two or three pictures on the strip.

TravelCard in hand, you are ready to explore. Riding the Tube — here, there, anywhere — is about the best and most important thing you could do at this point. For one thing, you can go pretty much anywhere you'd possibly want to using the Tube. For another, it hums with life, much like you'd imagine the inside of an anthill would. There are scads of people, all hustling down the throat-in-mouth-steep escalators and hurtling through the tunnels toward their platforms. At this point, it's not even necessary that you use the Underground to go anywhere. You just need to feel the energy of the Tube to take the pulse of London.

Perhaps, though, you should test your skills by plotting a way to Charing Cross Station, on the Northern and Bakerloo lines. You're heading to Trafalgar Square. Think of the Tube as London's arterial network and Trafalgar Square as its heart. Some might disagree — but they can write their own books. You'll find going places on the Tube to be amazingly simple. Armed with the handy pocket-sized Tube map that you should have been given when you bought your London TravelCard, and with a basic tourist map, you can go anywhere.

The Tube lines are represented by different colors and distinctive names. The Northern Line is black on your map, while the Bakerloo is brown. Nothing could be easier — the only thing that takes some getting used to is the fact that Londoners using the Underground tend to zip through its escalators and tunnels at speeds you've heretofore only associated with Olympic sprinters. Block the path of the perpetual hurriers, and you'll not only identify yourself as an ignorant tourist, but you may also get bowled over. Take fair warning — stand to the right on the escalators and keep moving in the tunnels. Don't panic if you get confused about which direction you are going or which platform you need. Underground line routes are posted at appropriate portals and turns, so you can always pause to get your bearings if you stay out of the path of other travelers. You are going to make a mistake or two with the Tube the first few days. Accept that and laugh about it when you do. Getting on the wrong Tube train or getting off at the wrong stop is easily remedied. Such a minor miscue just gives you a good story to tell at dinner. The ability to laugh at yourself and things that don't go as planned is vital to a successful stay abroad.

This time, though, you make it to Charing Cross Station without a hitch, and after you emerge from the Underground, you whip out your London map to figure out where Trafalgar Square is and, more to the point, where you are. We would wager that you never get the chance to actually locate your position on the map before some considerate soul asks you what you are looking for and puts you on the right path. Londoners can be extraordinarily helpful to visitors. You don't have to be lost. You don't even have to be looking at your map. You merely have to arch an eyebrow or stand too long in one spot to bring out the Good Samaritan in Londoners. We wouldn't be surprised if the person who comes to your rescue insists on walking you to Trafalgar Square just to make sure you arrive without misstep.

Trafalgar Square is bounded to the north by the National Gallery, a painting gallery that is one of the world's finest, if not *the* finest. From the portico of the National Gallery you have one of the most awe-inspiring views in London. In fact, that's one of the reasons you should come here at the start of your stay in London. Your eyes take in the majestic fountains whose figures spew and spurt arcs and jets of water, the statue of naval hero Lord Nelson atop its towering column, and, leading south from the square, Whitehall, a street lined with government ministries. You can just make out, at the edge of your field of vision, Big Ben, the clock tower of the Houses of Parliament. This view *is* London — the London you've always imagined.

Trafalgar Square is the place to begin orienting yourself. Mill around among the Londoners, mostly of the winged variety, and visitors who flock (excuse me) to the square. Look back toward the north. The dignified St. Martin-in-the-Fields Church pins down the northeast corner of the square. Make a mental note to go to the church at some point in your stay for one of the candlelight concerts for which it is renowned. Have a seat on one of the unforgiving stone benches at the edge of the square or on the lip of one of the glorious fountains. What's a little spray when you've got some daydreaming to do? You're in London after all, with weeks or months ahead of you. Watch the minidramas of the passersby and lingerers unfold: young lovers kissing by the fountains, kids scampering atop one of the enormous black iron lions at the base of Nelson's monument, snap-happy camera buffs, scavaging pigeons tempted by the promise of bird seed to perch on the arms or heads of laughing tourists. After you've had your fill of pigeons and people, go wherever you want. You have officially arrived in London.

In the coming days and weeks, you will get to know London better. The smartest thing that you can do for yourself is to walk as much as possible, particularly when you are going relatively modest distances. Sometimes the lure of the Underground and the double-decker buses is so strong that one is inclined to take public transportation everywhere. After all, you just plunked down lots of pounds for a TravelCard. We've both made the mistake before of spending the better part of a month down in the bowels of the Tube or on the second level of a bus. Don't misunderstand — those are terrificly convenient modes of transportation with significant cultural value, but you must let your feet guide you in equal measure. Each of these three ways of getting around — and you could add taxis for a fourth — provides its own unique perspective on London. In the early part of your stay, walking is particularly enlightening. For one thing, you begin to sketch in a mental map of the city. For another, you can always stop and gawk at interesting architecture or the array of umbrellas in the shop window or even the ragged street person politely asking for handouts. On second thought, it would be rude to gawk at him. Walking isn't just a way of getting around London, it's a way of getting to know London — to know its twists and turns, its sights and sounds, its colors and smells. London reveals its texture for the walker, who pieces together a vision and a sensibility of the city as a whole. The visitor who spurns footpower in favor of more mechanical means of transport will still have a marvelously rich experience, but he or she will miss out on something wonderful.

When you aren't engaged in class or some other academic endeavor, you should explore London. Trust us, there's no end of things to do. How you go about conquering the city is a highly individual thing. Some take as their starting point all the things they've heard of, so they begin checking sites off a master list of Must Sees: the Tower of London, the Houses of Parliament, the British Museum, Westminster Abbey. That's a tried-and-true approach. After all, presumably these places are famous for good reason and, besides, you don't want to be worried about not making it there. But there are other ways to experience London.

A great way to get to know the city is to simply choose an area on your map or from your guidebook and go see what it has to offer. Instead of focusing on a particular tourist attraction, turn your gaze on a particular part of the city. Unburdened by expectations, you are free to draw your own conclusions. We are both fond of this method of exploration. Sometimes you need an excuse to target an area. Take Chelsea, for example, sandwiched between the museums and department-store meccas of the South Kensington-Knightsbridge area and the Thames River. Sumptuous residences and quiet streets define Chelsea. While it bursts with character, Chelsea has no Tourist Temple at which travelers must pay homage. Granted there are a number of well-known

Chelsea attractions, but none on the order of Big Ben. You might have to rationalize devoting a couple of hours to Chelsea by wrapping your visit around something like lunch at a historic Chelsea pub recommended by your guidebook or a walk through the Physic Garden. *The Physic Garden?* you say. *You must be jesting!* But this is no ordinary garden. First of all, it dates to the 17th century, and any of you who have tried to keep a houseplant alive for more than three months can appreciate the miracle of plants that are three centuries older than you are. But more importantly, it gives you a corner of Chelsea to latch on to — it becomes a rationale for going. The joy of choosing an area of London and just going there to poke around is that you don't know what you'll find. At dinner everyone else will be talking about the same 10 places that have been the subject of discussion at every meal since you arrived. You, on the other hand, have the pleasure of watching their amazement when you announce that you spent your afternoon getting to know Chelsea, or Richmond, or Southwark. *But what did you do?* they ask. That's your cue for detailing your adventure.

You might also target particular experiences that would introduce you to certain aspects of the city, such as spending an afternoon wandering along the Thames, traversing each bridge you come to. You could see the London of the canals, exploring by foot and by canalboat. You could even spend an entire afternoon gazing at the city's sights from the top of a double-decker bus, changing routes whenever the mood strikes.

Themed exploration is another way of looking at

London. This week, you compare London's churches. Monday afternoon, you're rendered weak-kneed by Westminster Abbey; Tuesday, you gawk at St. Paul's Cathedral; Wednesday, it's the Brompton Oratory that you trek to; Thursday, the bells of Southwark Cathedral call your name; and Friday night, you go to the candle-light performance of Vivaldi's *Four Seasons* at St. Martin-in-the-Fields. Saturday seems an appropriate day to step into the 12th-century St. Bartholomew the Great. Sunday, for good measure, you attend a service at whichever church inspired you the most.

Themed exploration may be too focused, too linear, for most of you, but for others, it may provide a uniquely stimulating perspective on London. Themed exploration teems with possibilities. You could devote a few consecutive afternoons to London's verdant parks or its art museums. You could have a theatre week. You could spend a week exploring places connected with Sherlock Holmes. Monday, you could go to the Sherlock Holmes Museum, Tuesday, to the Sherlock Holmes Pub, Wednesday, to . . . . You get the picture.

The point is, there is no *one way* to see London. Be adventurous. Don't worry about going to all the places your guidebook awards three stars. Go to the ones that appeal to you. Beyond that, stretch the boundaries of your interests by going places and having experiences that you don't know whether you'd enjoy. Personal growth is an inevitable by-product of spending time abroad, and trying new things or going places you haven't a clue about can be a great catalyst to this growth. You might, for example, be somewhat aimless one week in your ongoing relationship with London. *Aimless?* you ask dubiously. Yes, aimless. Consider spending your free time in the company of different tripmates, going to the places that interest them. Don't involve yourself in destination selection. Just tag along. Besides the inevitability of getting to know London better and the probability of learning more about your own likes and dislikes, there's the possibility that your afternoon in the company of Margaret and Nancy or Ashok and Tim will be the start of a great friendship.

Making friends when you're studying abroad isn't difficult. First of all, if you're in a program, there are other people in your program with whom you are sharing an incredible adventure. Bonding with them is natural. You may have come to London with a friend or two. If you did, that's terrific — you've got a head start on the solo travelers in terms of companionship. But, whether you came to London alone or not, making new friends is an important part of the experience. Don't be afraid to strike up a conversation with your program-mates. If you're going to the Tower after class, invite a couple of people along. Alternatively, ask a few of them what they're doing and whether they would be amenable to your joining them. Unless you are unusually obnoxious or covered with scales, they will almost certainly welcome your company. Don't overdo it by continually forcing your company on the same people if they don't seem to be reciprocating. Depending on the size of your group, the possible permutations of interaction range from lots to something approaching infinity. In other words, don't be afraid to get to know people. There isn't that awkward lull in conversation that you can experience with new relationships at home because you can't run out of things to talk about in London — you are all seeing and doing an endless number of neat things, and you have so many neat stories to tell that the words will flow spontaneously. You are sharing an intense experience with these people, and bonding is inevitable. In fact, we'd be willing to wager that you will even befriend someone you wouldn't have imagined you could strike up a friendship with on your home campus. Some of the surface differences melt away or become less off-putting when you're abroad.

In addition to cultivating camaraderie with other students in your program, you should meet Londoners. After all, an intercultural experience is about much more than visiting museums and cathedrals. Meeting Londoners isn't difficult. Don't even *try*. Just open yourself up to the possibility. Most Londoners are polite to foreign visitors. Many Londoners regard foreigners with an affable curiousity — which is surprising since in midsummer sometimes it seems as if half the population of London is speaking Italian or Japanese or American-accented English. You'd think the sight of another ambulatory cultural *faux paus* would be enough to make a Londoner's blood boil, but Londoners are remarkably good hosts. You are most likely to meet locals if you are by yourself or in the company of just one other person. If you travel in packs, resign yourself to missing out on getting to know the natives.

But alone, or with a friend, you may meet Londoners in all kinds of circumstances. The pub is a great place to strike up a conversation or be drawn into one. Conversation is as much at the core of the pub experience as is beer — maybe more so. How the conversation gets started is hard to say. It just *happens* spontaneously. If you are of legal age and planning to have a beer or cider, ask the bartender or the person beside you what he recommends. Explain that you are a foreigner and don't have a clue about which one to try. This request always meets with earnest and caring assistance. We've seen a half-dozen people congregate around the bar debating what the foreign visitor should try, and when the foreigner finally makes a selection, they press him for a reaction. Five minutes later, the conversation is about royal scandals or politicians' peccadillos. The next time you walk into that establishment, you'll be warmly greeted by your new pals. Don't mistake a British pub for an American bar or a French bistro. The pub is very much about community, even in London. That sense of community is one reason you'll find so many people who are eager to exchange views with you. Just about anything will work as a conversation starter. Maybe one of the endless cricket matches is playing on the TV in the corner. Ask a simple question about the rules and you'll find yourself getting an hour-long introduction to the nuances of the sport.

The best area for meeting British students is Bloomsbury, home to the sprawling University of London. Students are everywhere in Bloomsbury — the pubs, cafes, bookshops. Two places where you are guaranteed to find British university students are the University Tavern on Store Street and the Student Union on Malet Street. Both are just minutes from Goodge Street Underground Station. Because these places cater to students, you'll find prices that please, particularly in the Student Union, where the upstairs cafeteria is not only remarkably cheap but, with its glass atrium, quite pleasant.

Many of our favorite moments in London relate to chance encounters with Londoners who have gone out of their way to tell us about their city, their country, their culture. When all is said and done, you'll probably remember more fondly that chat with the old carpenter who reminded you of your granddad or with the banker who told you how to achieve peace in Northern Ireland than you will the third cathedral or the fourth castle that you visit. Getting to know the people is as important — if not more important — a part of understanding London as is visiting the Houses of Parliament or St. Paul's Cathedral.

It's easy to get so caught up in seeing things that you forget to experience London. You can spend part of every day in London going somewhere famous, and yet you won't see everything, whether you're in London for a month or a year. There's just too much to do. You'll drive yourself nuts if you feel that you must see everything in your guidebook. The best advice is to keep busy, do what you most want to do, and take some time out for a breather now and then.

For example, head with a book or a couple of newspapers to Regent's Park and spend the afternoon reading and recharging your batteries. If it's summer, you'll find spectacular roses of vivid hues and heavenly scents. The park is also a prime spot for Frisbee — unless your lack of accuracy makes you a threat to passersby, and speaking from experience, there's nothing like an errant Frisbee to scatter a wedding party in the park! In the same vein, you can take the District Line to Kew, the next-to-the-last stop, and visit the Royal Botanical Gardens, replete with Victorian greenhouses and plants of every description.

You might go with a friend and pack a picnic lunch. A hunk of cheese, some slices of salami, a couple of apples, and a bottle of mineral water can go a long way toward restoring your travel equilibrium. Quiet reflection and a break from the noises of the city are vital to those of you who are in London for a significant chunk of time.

Don't try to see and do everything. Just have fun every day and don't lose track of the reason you're here — to learn . . . about London, about your field, and about yourself.

Chapter 7

Course Work? While I'm in London?

You've had a brief but immensely enjoyable introduction to London, but then reality intrudes. It's time to come to grips with the other reason that you're in London — to have a rich academic experience. Most of you are in London as part of a study experience arranged by a school or organization, and you have classes to attend. A few of you are in London doing independent study, which requires great self-motivation and diligence. By this point, you've realized that there's no end of history-drenched attractions, convivial pubs, eye-riveting art collections, lively pubs, ear-pleasing music venues, quaint and quiet pubs, architecturally inspiring buildings, and back-slapping-fun pubs. A few too many pubs in that sentence? Perhaps, but the point is — day or night — London teases visitors with its smorgasbord of pleasures. Anytime you're abroad, it's easy to succumb so completely to the charms of the place you're

visiting that you become sidetracked from study or business or whatever purposeful activity has taken you overseas. What you're looking for is balance.

Looking at London through the prism of your field of study, or really through any academic discipline, allows you to tap into the city and culture in a way that transcends the experiences of the casual visitor. You may be surprised to discover that learning can be so much fun.

Consider London to be a classroom on a grand scale. Everything that happens within the walls of the actual room or rooms where your classes meet, if you're in London on a formal program, should be amplified through experiences that are available on the streets and in the buildings of London and through contact with Londoners.

Your courses will likely have been designed with that in mind, but even if they were envisioned in the more limited way of the traditional campus courses, you can enrich the learning experience yourself by applying that principle.

Just as an example, let's consider some of the ways that we approach London as our classroom in the program we teach through the Department of Communication at the University of Dayton. One of our frequent offerings is *British Mass Media*. As part of the course unit on British newspapers, the class typically visits the headquarters of one of the country's major newspaper groups, and an executive provides an overview of the British newspaper industry. Afterward the students tour the newspaper facility and go to the newspaper printing plant, where they can see the newspapers rolling off the presses. On another occasion, the professor leads the students on a walking tour of Fleet Street, historically the nerve center of British journalism. Again the traditional classroom walls recede, but the learning continues in a more multidimensional way. In conjunction with the course unit on British television, the class attends the taping of a situation comedy for the British Broadcasting Corporation. That course unit is also supplemented through a visit to the offices of two or more television programming executives who typically intersperse programming clips with their remarks. Alternatively, a television executive may be invited to give a guest lecture at our classroom venue. Radio is covered through a guest lecture by a documentary producer for BBC Radio who plays snippets of BBC Radio documentaries. A guest lecturer from the British Film Institute or a British university often makes a presentation on contemporary British films. The film unit is augmented through a class outing to the cinema to view a contemporary British film. A visit to the Museum of the Moving Image, which traces the evolution of film and television in Britain, is often made.

In addition, hands-on exercises during a few classes allow students to become familiar with British newspapers and prompt the students to read these newspapers regularly on their own. During the television section of the course, the class typically meets at night once to watch several television programs and discuss how those programs differ from American ones in the same genre.

Lectures by the professor account for perhaps half of the course time. As you can see, students in the course are learning about British media in a variety of ways.

Assignments for the course require students to immerse themselves in some aspect of British media. They may involve reading a certain number of British newspapers and making a written comparison of British newspapers with American newspapers *vis-a-vis* the journalistic style, layout, advertising, and other factors. Assignments may require the students to watch a certain number of British television series in a particular genre and then write an essay comparing what they observed to American series in the same genre in terms of plot, dialogue, visual style, and other elements.

The course is shaped to ensure that students *experience* British media and *reflect* on what they observe, rather than just hear about them.

We're not trying to sell you any particular course here, but we think you should look for programs that fit their curricula to the location the way this course does.

If the program from your school *doesn't* do that, and you don't want to shop for another program, do it on your own by using the city as an extension of your class.

This approach can be used to enliven any course. It's a matter of educational philosophy more than of academic discipline. London has such a storied history and has been home to so many people who have played prominent roles in every field that there is no shortage of possibilities to enhance a course. Add to that the fact that London today is a dynamic capital with particular importance in communication, performing arts, literature, visual art and design, finance, and numerous other fields. Your professors ought to be able to design courses that take advantage of the virtually unlimited possibilities to inject color and insight into academic subjects. The question posed in this chapter's title may be misformulated. Maybe it should be called *Course Work? It Sounds Exciting! Besides, That's (Partly) Why I'm in London.*

Don't leave your education up to your professors entirely. Education is best acquired by curious minds. What the professors serve up on a platter may be the main dish, but what fine meal would be complete without the appetizer, salad, wine, dessert, and coffee? Whether your study-abroad course is cleverly conceived to use London as a classroom or one that delivers re-hashed campus material with little effort to take advantage of the city's offerings — God forbid! — you still have an important role to play.

Mindset is everything. Sometimes in school you feel like you're a prisoner of the classroom, of the course readings, of the material. You should never have that feeling when you are studying abroad. First, and foremost, studying abroad is by definition *fun*. Don't be afraid to enjoy your courses; in fact, embrace them. The routines of campus learning have been left behind. You're in another culture, and virtually every experience you have, whether in the classroom or at the greengrocer or on the Underground or via a conversation with a Brit, involves learning and cultural adaptation to some degree. You encounter so many things that are new and different in your environment and, consequently, in yourself, that studying abroad — heck, just being abroad — is an exhilarating experience. Besides, presumably you've enrolled in courses that interest you. The courses should be designed to take advantage of the site. The degree to which they are site specific will vary, of course, according to the course subject. If after a class or two you aren't inspired by the course, see if you can switch to another one. Don't be passive about your study-abroad experience.

Get involved. Ask questions in class or on field trips, even if you are unaccustomed to doing so at home. As an active participant, you'll get more out of the course. Read the course material. If anything, readings for a course abroad should have even more relevance than those for the same course or a similar course at home. They would likely refer to places, people, events, and phenomena with connections to the vibrant city that is your temporary home. Often course material and college life seem at odds. You're sitting in your dorm room in Austin, Texas, reading *Richard III* for your Shakespeare class the next day. Sixth Street, with its countless watering holes and music venues, beckons. You heed the siren call partly because Sixth Street is a lot of fun and partly because you're having a tough time envisioning the court intrigues in *Richard III*, notwithstanding the fact that Will wasn't a half-bad writer. Reading the same work for your literature or history or theatre course in London is another matter altogether. For one thing, you can bolster your imagination by visiting landmarks like the Tower that figure prominently in the drama. For another, you may be able to see the play itself, performed by the Royal Shakespeare Company at the Barbican or some other venue such as the Open Air Theatre in Regent's Park. Think about that art survey course that fulfills a college requirement. On campus you've got to stretch your imagination past the flat reproductions of the textbook or the slides shown in class. If you take the same course in London, you can actually see many of the paintings themselves, in all their glory, at the National Gallery, the Tate Gallery, the Courtauld Institute, or some other art museum. Suddenly the course material comes to life.

Your motivation to go beyond the requirements of a course and augment the learning experience through your own explorations will likely depend on why you're taking the course and how successful the instructor is at getting you excited about the material. If you're taking a course that's part of your major field of study or closely linked to it, you should already have all the motivation you need.

Embrace London with gusto, not just generally

speaking, but also in terms of what you're studying. Let's say hypothetically that you are an art major at home and enrolled in art courses in your London program. Seek out lesser-known galleries as well as the most famous. Buy a couple of British art magazines to acquaint yourself with the local scene and with the latest trends. Find out about exhibits and special lectures. Try to meet some British art students. Through these extra endeavors, you'll have a much richer experience, no matter how well the course is designed, and that experience will be heightened by a sense of pride about the part you play.

If you are a drama student taking a Shakespeare class in London, you'll probably get your fill of the Bard, but don't deny yourself the opportunity to explore other facets of the London theatre scene. Don't let everything be about credit hours and grades. Make sure you see a wide range of contemporary theatre as well, both in the West End and in the fringe-theatre category. Not only will it be educational and fun, but you'll wow your professor with clever comparisons of some contemporary drama with one by Shakespeare.

One of our communication students, an electronic-media major taking a British mass-media course and a general course on communication in Britain, decided to try to meet a number of British television and newspaper executives. Her aggressiveness paid off. Surprised by her moxie, they were glad to give her a half-hour of their time. She learned something about British media and the decision-making process of high-powered media executives, but she also learned a valuable lesson.

Rest assured that the other students who listened to her recounting her adventures were more than a little impressed, not to mention her professors. That is going the extra mile, but there are many easy and fun ways to enhance your learning in London.

The second part of this book is written with this approach in mind. Each chapter in the second part is devoted to elaborating on ways students of different subjects can customize their learning experience in London. We tell you about the out-of-the-way, largely overlooked place with great relevance to your field. We direct you to that little museum with eye-opening exhibits. We tell you where the discoverer of this and the founder of that actually worked, lived, or is buried.

How you utilize the second part depends on you. If you're a political-science major in London on a program dedicated to political science, then your focus is obviously Chapter 12. Maybe, however, you're a political-science major, but you've enrolled in a program through which you're taking one political-science course and one communication course. We hope you'll follow up on ideas in both Chapter 11 and Chapter 12 to try to squeeze as much out of your study abroad as possible.

What if you are an art major, but you enroll in an English-literature program offered by your university? Don't limit yourself to the literature chapter. Take advantage of being in London to do some independent learning about art.

You don't have to restrict yourself to what you are studying in your courses. How many times in your life will you be in London, with its almost limitless opportunities to enhance your understanding of any field, whether it's your major, or another field that you are interested in? So browse through the chapters in the second part of the book and take from them whatever you want.

Hold on a minute, you say. *I don't want to be always tied up with school.* We wouldn't want that either. Like we said before, the key is balance. We design our courses so that students have an interesting mix of traditional lectures, guest lectures by London professionals, professional site visits, museum visits, and other activities. And we suggest to our students other ways to enrich their study on their own. But we encourage them in equal measure to squeeze the most out of London in other respects as well.

So how do you do it all? How can you approach your courses with great enthusiasm, vigor, and a sense of exploration and still have energy and time to approach sightseeing and socializing with the same gusto? Good time management, adequate but not overindulgent sleep, and respect for your body.

Good time management means not spending inordinate amounts of time lounging around the dormitory, flat, or hotel room. A little down time is a very good thing, but even that can be put to good use with such activities as reading British newspapers, magazines, or books or leisurely reading your course materials. Come to think of it, the best time to do your course readings may be before you even arrive in London. Give serious thought to this suggestion. It's a great way to relieve time pressure. Thinking ahead a little about what you want to do the next day or over the weekend is a good way to avoid ending up wasting valuable hours of free time debating what to do. Riding back to your area of London on the Underground Sunday night is a great

time to reflect on what you'd like to do on Monday and Tuesday. The train ride from York back to London after a fabulous weekend spent exploring York Minster, the city walls, the Jorvik Viking Centre, and the medieval streets of the Shambles is a great time to catch up on course work — and the journal that we convinced you earlier to keep!

Not much needs to be said about sleep. If you don't get enough, obviously you'll be dragging the next day. Sure, you cut corners with sleep all the time back at school, but it's different when you're abroad. Your engine is revved up higher. Friday's guest lecture would be considerably more clever and inspiring on six hours of sleep than on four. A weekend in Scotland is a wonderful thing, but taking the overnight train on Sunday from Edinburgh to London means that you'll be hard-pressed to keep from flattening your nose on the table as you sit through Monday morning's classes. You then haul yourself to bed and sleep through the rest of the day or go zombie-like through whatever activities are scheduled either through your courses or with your friends.

Sufficient sleep isn't the only important consideration in taking care of yourself. You certainly won't get much out of your class field trip on Tuesday if you wake up with a hangover from the excessive number of pints you quaffed on Monday night at the Lord John Russell Pub. *But the pub represents local culture,* you respond with a nod and a wink. Right you are. Sure, David the publican can enlighten you about any aspect of local culture and the University of London students you've befriended, Rob and Scott, are fun to shoot the breeze with. But before you order that extra pint of Abbot Ale, look around. The vast majority of Brits go into the pub for a pint or two and an equal measure of conversation, going home an hour later with their wits intact. If you go to the pub for conversation first and drink second, you'll be fresher for the million other things that you should appreciate about London. Mineral water makes for a nice alternative on an occasional or regular basis, too, and doesn't detract in the least from the pleasures of the pub.

Taking care of your body also means eating well — you won't have the energy for anything if you aren't giving yourself enough sustenance. Most people find that their appetite is much bigger when they are abroad, racing around with a full shot of adrenaline coursing through their veins. Like we said earlier, studying abroad is exhilarating, and you typically use more energy than when you're at home. So plenty of healthy food is vital, not to mention the importance of paying attention to existing medical conditions, the onset of illness, and the like. Most study-abroad programs are fast-paced, and you are certainly going to be trying to pack an incredible number of activities into every week. That's why you want to take care of yourself. This is no time to neglect your body's needs.

Reasonable and useful advice, all of the above. The most important thing, however, is mindset. That's the real key to having both a rich academic experience and a rich touristic, cultural, and social experience. Approach your courses, as everything else, with a positive attitude and flexible spirit. Succeed in that and you'll go home intellectually and culturally nourished.

Remember,
for updates to this book, check our Web site at
http://www.as.udayton.edu/com/faculty/student.htm

Part II

In Search of the Head of Jeremy Bentham

In the chapters that follow, you'll find the favorite places of the authors, as well as of students, professors, and professionals, that relate to a wide variety of academic fields. Each chapter is organized in the same way, with the same general headings, as follows:

The London Experience is a true insider's view of the relationship between the subject and something that is quintessentially London. Sometimes it's an off-the-beaten-track walk, sometimes an experience you might not think of on your own, but it's always something that will give you the unique flavor of this unique city as it relates to the subject you are studying and experiencing.

On Display takes you to the one museum or exhibit in each field that you mustn't miss.

Cool Corners are one or more out-of-the-way places important to the topic that students seldom find for themselves — places altogether unique.

Street Study lets you walk with us through a part of London associated with the subject — a walk that will give you a deeper acquaintance with the place, the people, or the times that shaped your field.

Immersion puts you in position to soak up the special flavors of your subject as provided by London. These are fun things to see or do alone or with a friend — activities that would be difficult or impossible to do anywhere but London.

The Crown Jewels are the glittering guidebook attractions in your field that people come to London to see. We won't bore you with the details that more general guides offer about these places, but we do remind you they're there.

Sherlock Suggests is an assortment of places hunted down by the master sleuth himself — quick descriptions of special places you should know about.

By the way, if you read the entire book, sometimes we might seem to repeat ourselves. That's not because we're getting old and senile (well, maybe a little), but because lots of places in London pertain closely to more than one field of study. Always remember, though, that no matter what this or any other guidebook says, the *best* places in London are the ones *you* enjoy the most!

Chapter 8

Art, Architecture, and Music

London has been at the forefront of so many movements in art, architecture, or music through the centuries that any visitor to London ends up getting at least a barebones course in these fine arts. For the *student* of these disciplines, however, time in London should add a great deal of flesh to the bone.

THE LONDON EXPERIENCE
In Pursuit of Christopher Wren

No individual has had a greater hand in imposing an architectural vision on London than Christopher Wren. Newcomers to London become accustomed to hearing tour guides say something like: *St. Bob's, built by Christopher Wren in 1672, is considered the finest example of . . . .* His name pops up in conjunction with so many buildings that sometimes you want to scream: *Where were all the other architects? Were they wiped out by some bizarre virus that struck people who worked with blueprints?*

Wren must have been a busy man. The Great Fire of 1666 leveled the City of London almost as completely as if an atom bomb had been dropped on it. The Gothic St. Paul's Cathedral and 180 churches were among the four-fifths of the City that was destroyed. Wren set about redefining the City. He rebuilt St. Paul's and 51 churches in the City, twenty-three of which survive. Wren's impact goes beyond the City as well — he redesigned Kensington Palace for King William and Queen Mary, who took up residence in 1690. He played a major role in shaping nearby Greenwich, designing a number of structures, including the Old Royal Observatory and what is today the Royal Naval College.

Since Christopher Wren's designs figure so prominently in London today, three centuries after he realized them, pursuing Wren's vision is the perfect London experience for students with interests in architecture. You can approach this in various ways. We recommend that you go about it slowly and systematically, perhaps designating one week as Wren Week.

On Sunday, go to **St. Paul's Cathedral** (LUDGATE HILL; ST. PAUL'S UNDERGROUND). A great way to appreciate St. Paul's is to attend a service. Experiencing St. Paul's as a house of God, rather than as a tourist attraction, allows you to better understand Wren's design and what he was trying to achieve architecturally. Afterward, head out for some lunch, returning later to take a tour of St. Paul's or wander around on your own. (THERE'S MORE ABOUT ST. PAUL'S IN CHAPTER 9.)

You can visit **St. Bride's** (FLEET STREET; BLACKFRIARS UNDERGROUND) on Monday. Wren rebuilt this church, known as the journalists' church, from 1670 to 1684. St. Bride's is perhaps best known for its steeple, which rises in stages so gracefully that it inspired a local baker to mimic the design for wedding cakes, thus establishing a tradition that survives to this day.

On Tuesday, go to the **Monument** (MONUMENT STREET; MONUMENT UNDERGROUND), which stands as a reminder of the Great Fire. The Monument, finished in 1677, is 202 feet high because the fire began 202 feet from this spot. You can walk up the 311 steps of the internal spiral staircase to reach a viewing platform that affords rather extraordinary views despite the protective cage that keeps people from taking a plunge. A visit to the Monument is an important reminder of the destruction that made it necessary for so much of the City to be rebuilt.

Visit **St. Mary-le-Bow** (CHEAPSIDE; ST. PAUL'S OR MANSION HOUSE UNDERGROUND) on Wednesday. This church, rebuilt by Wren from 1670 to 1683 of Portland stone, is famed for its spire and bells.

Thursday, go to **Hampton Court Palace** (BY BRITISH RAIL FROM WATERLOO STATION). Wren built the east wing and part of the south wing, as well as the Banqueting House and State Apartments. A highlight is Fountain Court, which the State Apartments overlook.

You should be up for another church on Friday. Go see **St. Stephen Walbrook** (WALBROOK; CANNON STREET UNDERGROUND), where Wren tried out some of his architectural notions before applying them to St. Paul's.

Travel to nearby **Greenwich** (RIVERBUS OR DOCKLANDS LIGHT RAILWAY ARE SCENIC OPTIONS) on Saturday to see two Wren designs, the Royal Naval College and Flamsteed House, part of the complex of buildings that made up the Old Royal Observatory. Wren built Flamsteed House as a residence for John Flamsteed, the first royal astronomer.

If you have sightseeing stamina, you might go for two Wren sites each day — these are countless, so you wouldn't have any trouble adding more. Alternatively, you could go to one a week — everything depends on your taste and the duration of your stay in London.

Another approach would be to take in as much Wren as you can in one fell swoop. If that's more to your liking, consider taking a guided walking tour offered by The Original London Walks (telephone: 0171-624-3978). There is an Original London Walk entitled *Christopher Wren's London*. For a few pounds you can cover a lot of ground, both physically and informationally. This is such an effortless way — ok, so there's a bit of walking, but you've got strong, young legs — to gain perspective on Wren that you might want to do this as part of the daily site approach outlined above.

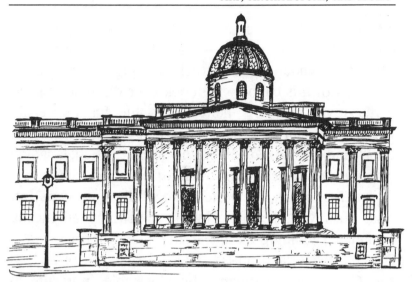

ON DISPLAY
The National Gallery

A museum that figures near the top of almost anyone's must-see list in London is the **National Gallery** (TRAFALGAR SQUARE; CHARING CROSS UNDERGROUND), but for art students the National Gallery is such a treasure trove that you should visit time and time again. It is so central to the studies of an artist or artist-to-be that the National Gallery should open a youth hostel in the basement so that you could roll out of bed and get right to it. Without a doubt, the National Gallery is one of the finest painting galleries in the world — if not the finest.

Enter the original 19th-century building at the north side of Trafalgar Square, pick up a gallery plan, and begin your visual exploration. There is no charge for admission, so the painting perusal begins on an optimistic note!

We often start with the galleries dedicated to Impressionism. Renoir's *The Umbrellas*, Van Gogh's *Sun-flowers*, Seurat's *Bathers* — the admirer of Impression-istic art is rendered dumbstruck at being able to gaze at paintings of this caliber. No book ever did them justice. Perhaps you're more interested in the Italian Renais-sance. You can see the Da Vinci cartoon *Virgin and Child* and his *Madonna of the Rocks*, Michelangelo's *Entombment,* and works by Botticelli, Del Sarto, and Titian. Maybe Dutch masters (hopefully not cigars) are what push your aesthetic button. Then, by all means, commune with works by Rembrandt, Vermeer, Van Dyck, Rubens, and others. Don't forget you're in Brit-ain. Check out landscapes by Constable, portraits by Reynolds. There are some magnificent paintings by Gainsborough and Turner.

The only drawback to the National Gallery is that there is so much to see — the history of art meticulously unfolds, canvas after glorious canvas — that you can be easily overwhelmed. Systematically seeing the artworks in one visit would likely take you six hours. Remember, you aren't training for a museum marathon. You're here to SEE, REFLECT, SEE, DIGEST, SEE, PONDER. Note that we didn't include SEE, PASS OUT. Therefore, it is impor-tant that you take in the National Gallery in reasonable chunks of time.

The newer Sainsbury wing of the National Gal-lery has a cafe that affords one of the finest views in London and provides a great setting for refreshment and reflection. If you are planning a multi-hour visit, break it up with an interlude in this pleasant cafe.

COOL CORNERS

Wigmore Hall (36 WIGMORE STREET; BOND STREET OR OXFORD CIRCUS UNDERGROUND): A Sunday morning concert at Wigmore Hall is an extraordinary experience that is guaranteed to soothe the soul of visitors to London. The Wigmore has a terrific year-round slate of concerts, but the summer Sunday morning coffee concerts, which start at 11:30 A.M., are a special treat. We suggest you arrive at least a half-hour earlier, *The Sunday Times* or another quality British newspaper in hand, and savor your morning coffee in the downstairs cafe while you take stock of world happenings. That sets the tone nicely for the event that follows.

Wigmore Hall is so breathtakingly ornate that the modest admission price would seem reasonable even if the musicians never showed up. But show up they do — world-class pianists, string quartets, vocalists, and musical ensembles of various configurations gracefully fashion melodies that enfold you, enter you, and erase the cares and concerns of travel and study.

After the concert, exchange your ticket for a cup of coffee or a glass of sherry. Even if you go alone — and sometimes it is next to impossible to coax anyone into meeting you on Sunday morning — you are likely to find yourself in a conversation with another concertgoer. The whole experience is, well, rather civilized.

The Courtauld Institute Galleries (SOMERSET HOUSE, THE STRAND; CHARING CROSS UNDERGROUND): The vast majority of visitors to London bypass the Courtauld in favor of bigger, better-known art museums such as the National Gallery or the Tate Gallery. If they only knew what they were missing! Nothing about a visit to the Courtauld feels *obligatory*. The museum is the perfect size so that you aren't overwhelmed. Never does one think: *Gee, how many more galleries are there?* You can go through the Courtauld at a leisurely pace and really think about what you are seeing. Another factor that aids in this pleasurable viewing is the fact that the Courtauld is typically uncrowded, so you don't have to elbow your way through a pack of people clustered around each painting.

On the occasion of his first visit to the Courtauld, one of the authors had the experience of coming face to face with Monet's *Impression, Sunrise*, on loan from another museum. The name of the movement Impressionism was taken from this artwork. Imagine standing in a small gallery, alone, gazing enraptured at *Impression, Sunrise* for 10 minutes, undisturbed by any other museum visitor. No ninny bumping into you with a video camera. No forbidden flashes blinding you and potentially damaging the paintings while a security guard pays no heed. No annoyingly loud gawker braying: *Fred, isn't that the same picture we saw done in that lovely velveteen at Kmart?* Instead, there was solace and the rare opportunity to move around the room and view the painting from different angles and varying distances. You could not enjoy a painting that famous in such serenity in the National Gallery in London or the Louvre in Paris or the Metropolitan Museum of Art in New York. The intimacy of the setting makes for a special experience.

One of the highlights of a visit to the Courtauld is

seeing Manet's *Bar at the Folies-Bergere*. The wide-ranging collection has works from Botticelli, Rubens, Renoir, Van Gogh, and 20th-century British artists. If you're a fan of the Impressionists, this is the best place in London to see them — even better than the National Gallery. The only drawback to the Courtauld is that the lack of air-conditioning makes for a rather sweaty visit on a hot summer day.

Somerset House itself is impressive. The Courtauld Galleries occupy just part of this enormous 18th-century stone building, which also houses a variety of government offices.

STREET STUDY
The Banks of the Thames

Sometimes it's easy to overlook how vital the Thames is to London and how prominently the river figures in the urban design. Take the Underground to Westminster Station. When you emerge into Parliament Square, take a few minutes to appreciate the elegant grandeur of the Houses of Parliament. Sir Charles Barry designed the **Houses of Parliament**, built in the mid-19th century in the late Gothic style. Gaze at the clock tower nicknamed Big Ben that has come to symbolize London. Facing the square is the 11th-century Westminster Hall, which Barry seamlessly incorporated into his design for Parliament. Although other architectural sirens are on or around this square — St. Margaret's Church and Westminster Abbey chief among them — the river calls.

Take Bridge Street, the street bordering the

111

Houses of Parliament on the north, until you get to **Victoria Embankment,** just before Westminster Bridge. From this spot you will get a wonderful view of the Houses of Parliament. You may even want to cross the bridge halfway or entirely, but if you do, return back across and walk north along Victoria Embankment. Gazing across the river, your attention is captured by the early 20th-century **Old County Hall**, which served as the home to the Greater London Council, now defunct.

Walk along the Victoria Embankment, past **Cleopatra's Needle**, to Waterloo Bridge. As you walk, notice not only the needle, an Egyptian obelisk, circa 1450 BC, that was put here in 1878, but also the benches whose decorative ends evoke Egypt. After admiring the needle and ironwork of the benches and lampposts, gaze across the Thames at the repugnant concrete structures on the South Bank.

The cluster of buildings, which you might at first mistake for parking garages or above-ground nuclear-blast shelters, are in fact cultural facilities. This concrete nightmare comprises the **South Bank Centre**, which includes the Royal Festival Hall, the Queen Elizabeth Hall, and the Purcell Room; the **National Film Theatre;** the **Hayward Gallery;** the **Museum of the Moving Image;** and the **Royal National Theatre.** Architecturally, these buildings lack grace and fail to inspire. Perhaps you recall the flap surrounding Prince Charles' reference to a design for the Sainsbury wing of the National Gallery as a "carbuncle." By comparison, these buildings represent hemorrhoids on the buttocks of the

Thames. You'd be hard-pressed to find many people, Londoners and visitors alike, who would speak favorably of the architecture. Certainly, London isn't the only city disfigured by modernist architecture of the 50s and 60s — in fact, much of Eastern Europe suggests a concrete mixers' conspiracy — but London is filled with so many elegant or imposing or intriguing structures of different eras that one must be appalled at the assault on the senses represented by these singularly unattractive buildings.

Walk across Waterloo Bridge and take a closer look at this architectural folly. The South Bank Centre, National Film Theatre, and Hayward Gallery are on the west side of the bridge, while the Royal National Theatre and Museum of the Moving Image are on the east side. While you are in London, try to visit all of these places individually. All have interesting offerings, and you really should see the inside to better understand the architectural vision — or lack thereof.

Continue east along the river, past Blackfriars Bridge, until you come to the site of the re-creation of the **Globe Theatre**. A tour of the Globe provides not

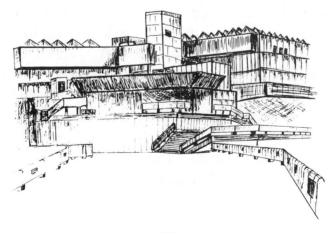

only insight into theatre in Shakespeare's day, but it also informs you about theatre architecture in Elizabethan times. You've gone from the concrete jungle to the domain of the woodworker. What contrast!

You could very well be in need of a refreshing pause at this point. Continue east on the Bankside until you see the **Anchor Bankside Tavern**, a wonderful historic watering hole with a fine selection of ales and decent pub grub. Weather permitting, take your beverage onto the Anchor's brick terrace and sit at one of the picnic tables overlooking the Thames. You can further reflect on architecture while taking in the cityscape across the river. Prominent in the view is the dome of St. Paul's Cathedral.

When you leave the Anchor, head away from the river via Bank Street, from which you quickly take a right on Clink Street, which feeds into Cathedral Street. Did we lose you? That's okay. We've lost our bearings here too, and that doesn't have to be frustrating — it can lead to great discoveries. Anyway, Cathedral Street is aptly named because it leads you to **Southwark Cathedral**. You didn't think we'd take you on an architectural tour that didn't include at least one church, did you? Spend some time studying this overlooked Gothic jewel. Part of the church dates to the early part of the 13th century. The nave was rebuilt late in the 19th century.

Given that you've just visited the Globe recreation, you might be interested to note that William Shakespeare's brother Edmund is buried here at Southwark Cathedral. Another familiar name with a Southwark connection is Harvard — as in Harvard University. John Harvard, who founded the prestigious university in Cambridge, Massachusetts, was baptized in this church in 1607.

One of the best things about visiting the beautiful Southwark Cathedral is that you are likely to have the place pretty much to yourself. Most visitors to London quench their church thirst with Westminster Abbey and St. Paul's Cathedral. Few make it to Southwark Cathedral. (THERE'S MORE ABOUT THIS CHURCH AND AREA IN CHAPTER 10.)

Head back toward the Thames and walk east along the river, past London Bridge, until you come to **Hay's Galleria**, a shopping complex that reinvigorates old architecture with new purpose.

This 1980s urban renewal project was designed around the 1856 Hay's Wharf. A 90-foot iron-and-glass atrium lends an elegant touch to the old wharf, where upscale shops and cafes have replaced ships' cargos. While in this vicinity of the river, don't miss the opportunity for a good view of Tower Bridge and, across the Thames, the Tower of London.

Your walk completed, you might take advantage of the opportunity to relax awhile at a sidewalk cafe at Hay's Galleria. Even the most energetic traveler needs to find time to take it easy.

IMMERSION

Do I hear £2000?

The two most-storied auction houses in the world, Christie's and Sotheby's, both have London offices. Attending an auction at one of them gives you a glimpse of the world of the upper crust. You'll also see some beautiful or unusual and probably very expensive art, furniture, or whatever's being auctioned off that day in an atmosphere very different from that of a museum.

Both **Christie's** (8 KING STREET; PICCADILLY CIRCUS OR GREEN PARK UNDERGROUND) and **Sotheby's** (35 NEW BOND STREET; BOND STREET UNDERGROUND) have auctions that are open to the public. They don't check your wallet when you enter to ensure that you can afford the offerings. The only difficult aspect to attending an auction at one of these houses is that you need to restrain yourself from scratching your itchy nose or using your pointer to indicate to your companion something that you find interesting. Those sorts of gestures may be misinterpreted by the caller as bids on your part. Keeping your movements in check doesn't sound too hard, but when you know you shouldn't scratch, everything itches, and when you know you shouldn't point or wave your arms, suddenly the non-verbal aspects of your communication multiply. Ah, well. That Constable painting we bought looks great in our university department office, but tuition had to be doubled for communication majors, and the photocopier and fax machine had to be taken to the pawn shop.

THE CROWN JEWELS

St. Martin-in-the-Fields (ST. MARTIN'S LANE; CHARING CROSS UNDERGROUND): This beautifully austere church, which sits in the northeast corner of Trafalgar Square, fills up for candlelight performances of accessible classical favorites such as Vivaldi's *Four Seasons.*

The Tate Gallery (MILLBANK; PIMLICO UNDERGROUND): The Tate, which opened in 1897, specializes in British artists born before 1860 and artists of all nationalities born after that date. The highlights include an inspired group of paintings by Turner, Waterhouse's ethereal *Lady of Shalott,* and a collection of William Blake prints.

The Victoria and Albert Museum (CROMWELL ROAD; SOUTH KENSINGTON UNDERGROUND): The six miles of galleries in the Victoria and Albert contain a vast assortment of items, but the focus is on applied art. To try and see it all in one day would be suicidal. (THERE'S MORE ABOUT THE V&A IN CHAPTER 14.)

Royal Albert Hall (KENSINGTON ROAD; SOUTH

KENSINGTON UNDERGROUND): This domed brick building, just across the road from the Albert Memorial, is the site of a wide variety of musical events, including the summer Promenade Concerts, popularly known as the Proms.

SHERLOCK SUGGESTS . . .

Kenwood House (HAMPSTEAD; HAMPSTEAD UNDERGROUND): Kenwood House not only can boast of a fine collection of 17th- and 18th-century artwork, including paintings by Dutch masters Rembrandt and Vermeer and British artists Gainsborough and Raeburn, but it also hosts a well-regarded concert series in the summer.

Royal Academy of Arts (PICCADILLY; GREEN PARK OR PICCADILLY CIRCUS UNDERGROUND): The Royal Academy of Arts, in Burlington House, is the site of major art exhibits such as the Summer Exhibition as well as smaller ones. The grand facade of the 18th-century Burlington House incorporates statues of Da Vinci, Raphael, and others.

Heinz Gallery (21 PORTMAN SQUARE; MARBLE ARCH UNDERGROUND): This gallery has exhibits focusing on architecture.

William Morris Gallery (WALTHAMSTOW; WALTHAMSTOW CENTRAL UNDERGROUND): The gallery is located in Elm House, where the designer was born in 1834. The gallery traces Morris' career and contains examples of his work in wallpaper, rugs, carpets, ceramics, and other media.

Crypt of St. Paul's Cathedral (ST. PAUL'S

UNDERGROUND): The final resting place of Turner, Reynolds, and other painting luminaries is Painters Corner in the crypt of St. Paul's Cathedral. Memorialized are Constable, Blake, Van Dyck, and others. Architecture students won't want to miss the tombstone of Sir Christopher Wren in another area of St. Paul's crypt.

Sir John Soane's Museum (13 LINCOLN'S INN FIELDS; CHANCERY LANE UNDERGROUND): This museum, in the home of the famous architect who designed the Bank of England, highlights Soane's collection of art works. Unusual design elements of the house reflect Soane's eccentricities and sense of humor.

Fenton House (HAMPSTEAD; HAMPSTEAD UNDERGROUND): Music students shouldn't miss the collection of 17th- and 18th-century keyboard instruments at this 17th-century merchant's house. Concerts are held at Fenton House in the summer.

Guildhall (OFF GRESHAM STREET; MONUMENT OR BANK UNDERGROUND): The 15th-century Guildhall, whose name derives from its origins as a meeting hall of medieval guilds (the predecessors of unions), is the seat of government for the City of London. One doesn't usually think of music when one thinks of the Guildhall, but this was the site of the last public performance by Polish composer Frederic Chopin. A statue by the Festival Hall marks the occasion.

Ronnie Scott's (FRITH STREET; TOTTENHAM COURT ROAD OR LEICESTER SQUARE UNDERGROUND): Among the finest night clubs in London, Ronnie Scott's is a great jazz venue where the music takes precedence over the decor. The ambiance is pleasant, the music usually first-rate.

119

Hard Rock Cafe (150 OLD PARK LANE; HYDE PARK CORNER UNDERGROUND): Admittedly Hard Rock Cafes have spread like weeds across the globe, but the London Hard Rock is well worth a visit. After all, this is the *original* Hard Rock Cafe. It opened in 1971. The fare is simple but tasty and the portions huge. Devour barbeque ribs while surrounded by evocative rock memorabilia.

Musical Museum (368 HIGH STREET, BRENTFORD; GUNNERSBURY UNDERGROUND): This museum, inside what was once St. George's Church, features musical instruments such as pianos and organs that play automatically.

Royal College of Music (PRINCE CONSORT ROAD; SOUTH KENSINGTON UNDERGROUND): Across from the Royal Albert Hall is the Royal College of Music, built in 1893. The college houses the Museum of Instruments.

Royal Opera House (BOW STREET; COVENT GARDEN UNDERGROUND): This 1860 building is the home of both the Royal Opera and the Royal Ballet.

Rock Circus (PICCADILLY CIRCUS; PICCADILLY CIRCUS UNDERGROUND): If your musical interests run toward rock, you might check out this wax museum. You'll put on headphones and take a stroll through the history of rock music. Brace yourself — the sound system is poor and the entire experience rather contrived.

Chapter 9

Philosophy and Religion

Visitors usually expect Britain to be a very religion-oriented place. After all, its most famous king clashed with the pope and established his own church so he could marry his girlfriend; the monarch still is not only head of state but the head of the official state religion as well. England has been home to some of Christendom's most famous saints and martyrs and is where some of its grandest churches can be found.

Moreover, many mainline Protestant religions besides the Anglican/Episcopal Church got their start here. Britain is the home of John Wesley and Methodism. The preaching of French theologian John Calvin grew into the Scottish national religion of Presbyterianism and eventually gave rise to the dissenters who revolted against King Charles I and cut off his head. So they take their religion seriously in Britain, don't they?

Well, not exactly.

There is a deep respect for religious thought in Britain, but when it comes to the *practice* of religion, the British are, well, out of practice. As few as 15 percent of the population call themselves regular churchgoers, and it's not uncommon for tourists to far outnumber parishioners at Sunday services in famous cathedrals.

Don't be misled, however. The British may not practice while their clergy preaches, but the traditional values of the Christian faith have long been thoroughly integrated into the secular life of the island. Moreover, if you're here to study Western religious or philosophical thought, you'll have plenty to see and do. Non-Western religious traditions are also well represented, and London has significant populations of Muslims and Hindus, as well as a thriving Jewish community.

THE LONDON EXPERIENCE

Before Wren

London had the great misfortune to burn more or less to the ground a bit over 300 years ago, but the residents, although annoyed, used that mischance to construct some of the many familiar London landmarks we know today. Chief among the builders of post-fire London was a mathematician and amateur scientist and architect named Christopher Wren, whom you might have met in Chapter 8.

Everyone knows of the fabulous Wren churches. The last chapter discussed many of his greatest creations, St. Paul's Cathedral chief among them, but visitors almost always overlook the handful of lovely, even spectacular, churches that remain from before the Great Fire. Come with us, then, as we show you the churches that everyone else rushes past on their way to St. Paul's — the churches that were there *before* Christopher Wren.

Our walk begins, as so much else has, at the Tower of London. Inside the Tower is the church of **St. Peter ad Vincula** — St. Peter in Chains — burial place of those beheaded in the Tower, usually nobles or *former* friends of the monarch. It is open to visitors only for Sunday morning services or as part of the free tour from the Yeoman Warders of the Tower. In the White Tower is the peaceful **Chapel of St. John the Evangelist**.

Leave the Tower and move west, across Tower Green, site of the executions of less royally favored miscreants, to Byward Street. Here you'll find **All Hallows by the Tower.** Much of the upper portion of the church was rebuilt after World War II, but fragments of a Saxon church from about the year 700 were found during the reconstruction. The crypt dates from the 14th century and incorporates pavement that is more than 1900 years old.

Cross busy Byward Street and walk up Seething Lane. Just as you pass Pepys Street (named for one of the most famous residents of the area; we'll discuss him in detail in Chapter 15) on the right, look to your left at **St. Olave's Church.**

The original church on this site was built in 1050, before the Norman Invasion; this one dates from 1405. It was, in fact, Pepys' own parish church and stepping

in here on a hot day is like stepping into a cool cave. It's normally dark and the noise of the City sounds very far away — centuries away! But don't miss the churchyard. Its prison-like entrance is decorated with skulls and bones, and Dickens, in *The Uncommercial Traveller*, refers to the church as "St. Ghastly Grim." If you can't enter the church through the churchyard door, walk around to the north side of the building, on Hart Street, and find the main entrance.

When you leave, go west on Hart Street to the next street, Mark Lane, and turn right. You'll see a lonely stone tower, all that's left of the 15th-century church of **All Hallows, Staining.** It, too, survived the Great Fire, but it collapsed in 1671, according to parish records, because the church was undermined by too many graves next to its foundation. Elizabeth I attended services of thanksgiving here in 1554, before she became queen but after her sister, Queen Mary — "Bloody" Mary — released her from prison in the Tower.

At the next corner, turn right onto Fenchurch Street and walk up a short way until it joins Aldgate and Leadenhall Street. The Aldgate Pump, one of the original City pumps, still stands here. Turn left on Leadenhall Street, where there are two pre-fire churches. On the right-hand side will be **St. Katherine Cree** (1628), a

Gothic structure. A block farther on, set back a bit from the street, is **St. Andrew Undershaft** (built before 1520), whose name comes from the Maypole shaft which used to stand in front of it. We like this church because of its memorial to John Stow (1523–1605), whose survey of London was essentially the first travel guide to the City. The Lord Mayor puts a fresh quill in the hand of Stow's effigy each year. Colleague, we salute you! This church is presently undergoing restoration and is administered by the remarkable church we'll visit next.

Turn right on St. Mary Axe Avenue. A small lane, Undershaft, on the left will take you to a truly memorable medieval church, **St. Helen's Bishopsgate.** This wonderful church is one of the jewels of the City and worth spending a few more words on. St. Helen's is really two churches in one. Near an existing parish church, a nunnery was built about 1210, with an attachment on the original church for the use of the nuns. The parish church and the nun's church were separated by a screen. The convent was dissolved by Henry VIII in 1538, and the last of its buildings was torn down in 1799, although the enlarged church remained. About 1550 the screen separating the two halves of the church was pulled down, and the "double church" acquired its present, more open look. But remnants of its elder days survive. Be sure to look for the "nuns' squints" near the northeast corner. These angled slots allowed nuns who were unable to come into church the opportunity to watch church services from the outside of the building.

The church is so filled with monuments and memorials that it is sometimes called "the Westminster Abbey of the City." One you should be sure to look for is a window in the north wall dedicated to William Shakespeare. Even few Shakespeare devotees know that he must have once lived nearby because he was listed as a member of this parish in 1597.

The next stop should be just slightly north of St. Helen's on Bishopsgate. The tiny church of **St. Ethelburga,** more than 700 years old, was the smallest in the City, but it was badly damaged by terrorists in 1993. Tucked between modern office buildings, its future is uncertain and there's nothing to see now but scaffolding and plastic sheets.

Walk south on Bishopsgate, going past Threadneedle Street, until you reach the intersection with Cornhill. We're supposed to be talking about pre-fire churches here, but you ought to take a look at one Wren church now, **St. Peter's Cornhill,** which stands on what is supposed to be the location of the first Christian church in London, built before the year 550 according to one legend. Felix Mendelssohn himself played the organ at the current church. If you need a break for a few minutes, after you proceed west up Cornhill past St. Michael's, another Wren church, duck 'round the corner into an alley that leads to the **Jamaica Wine House**, a pub now but in 1657 the site of London's first coffee house. Note: if you enjoy the Maze at Hampton Court, you'll love wandering around in the little alleys here.

There's one more "church" on this part of our walk. If you walk down Cornhill past Mansion House, the home of London's Lord Mayor, and turn left onto

Queen Victoria Street, you'll reach London's oldest place of worship, the ruins of the **Temple of Mithras,** built by the Romans about the year 90.

At this point, you might want to interrupt your walk for a ride. While you can walk from here to our last three churches in no more than 15 or 20 minutes, it might feel good to sit down for a minute. Our next stop is about a £3 taxi ride away, or you can walk back up to Mansion House and jump on a No. 8, 22B, 25, or 501 bus and tell the driver to let you off at Bart's.

Bart's is St. Bartholomew's Hospital, and you'll get off the bus at Giltspur and Newgate streets. Right there is **St. Sepulchre-without-Newgate.** Newgate was a notorious and quite horrible prison that stood near here from 1180 to 1902. The church dates to before 1450, and for centuries the tolling of its bell was the last sound heard by victims of the many executions at the prison.

Now walk up the right-hand side of Giltspur to an opening for the car park at the hospital. A sign points to **St. Bartholomew the Less.** Walk through the gate and enter the cheerful, intimate little church with just seven pews on each side of the aisle. This lovely octagonal church has a wonderful vaulted ceiling, and its relatively large windows behind the altar give it a feeling of openness.

We may have saved the best for last. Turn right after you leave the hospital gate and walk another block, following the signs to **St. Bartholomew the Great.** It really *is* great! Parts of this church appear to date from the 1100s and it had its present form by the early 1500s. The church is a striking combination of bare stone and dark wood — cool, dim, and silent — with a pervasive feeling of great age like almost nowhere else in this ancient city. It is simultaneously uplifting and humbling to be in this place, and it is a fitting end to our pre-fire church walk. We've run out of churches, and after this one, anything else would be anticlimactic.

ON DISPLAY
The Holiest Place in England

Each hour one of the priests of **Westminster Abbey** (BROAD SANCTUARY; WESTMINSTER UNDERGROUND) climbs the steps of the pulpit, asks for quiet, and recites a prayer, reminding the hundreds of visitors that the Abbey isn't really a museum, it is a house of worship. The reminder is necessary because the Abbey, besides being one of the most important Christian churches in the world, *is* one of London's most marvelous museums, and too few of its visitors remember to treat it as a house of prayer and the holiest place in England.

Parts of the church are more than 900 years old, and the site has probably been a place of worship for very much longer than that. The realm's most solemn ceremonies, from the coronation of the monarch to important funerals like that of Princess Diana, are held here. Except at such times it is open to worshipers and visitors from Britain and around the world who come to view the tombs of many of Britain's kings and queens, the breathtaking architecture of the Henry VII Chapel, and the graves of saints.

We won't repeat the reams of information you'll get from even mediocre guidebooks; the glories of the Abbey are well documented and no visitor should miss them. Besides, in many of this book's chapters, we refer you to the Abbey to visit the gravesite or memorial of this scientist or that poet. Students in almost every field have an academic reason to come here, and once here, unless they are hopelessly befogged from their studies of pub culture, will stay to see the wonders of the place.

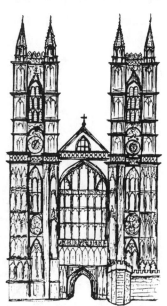

For students of religion or philosophy, at least, we suggest you come back on Sunday morning. The chief service, the Abbey Eucharist, is celebrated from the high altar at 11:15 A.M. and is accompanied by the famous Abbey choir — 12 adult professional musicians and 22 choristers, boys 8 to 13 years of age from the Abbey Choir School. When the service reaches *The Lord's Prayer*, listen for the echoes of the millions of voices that have recited those words in this sacred place over the past millennium. This has been the church of England's greatest kings and knaves, of its most sainted and scurrilous inhabitants, of the rich man and the beggar. Your visit will probably not be immortalized in the stones that commemorate so many others, but it will be an hour you are unlikely to forget.

COOL CORNERS

University College (GOWER STREET; EUSTON SQUARE UNDERGROUND): Here it is — the head of Jeremy Bentham. Bentham (1742–1832) was one of the most influential of modern philosophers. He developed the theory of Utilitarianism, later popularized by John Stuart Mill. A provision in Bentham's will called for his body to be preserved and, dressed in his favorite clothes and seated

in his favorite chair, exhibited at University College, where — since he left the College a lot of money — it can be seen to this day. The head was stolen as a college prank decades ago and since its recovery is kept in a box under the chair. A wax replica now sits atop Jeremy's body.

Enter the main gate of University College, which is a few blocks north of the British Museum on Gower Street. Enter the building by the door in the far right-hand (southeast) corner of the quadrangle. You'll find Jeremy in a large wood and glass display case on the ground floor just inside the entrance. Note that the case is shut up when school is not in session from early July until mid-September.

Postman's Park (LITTLE BRITAIN STREET; ST. PAUL'S UNDERGROUND): You're not likely to find this tiny green space unless you're looking for it. London taxi drivers know how to get *everywhere*, but the last one we asked to bring us here had to be directed to it. The St. Paul's Underground Station (CENTRAL LINE) brings you to street level at the conjunction of three major streets: Newgate, Cheapside, and St. Martin's Le Grand. Go north on St. Martin's a block or so until you cross Angel Street. On your left you'll find the church of St. Botolph Aldersgate. Its former churchyard is now Postman's Park, a green and quiet island that is a celebration of the heroism of the common man.

Nearly all religious and philosophical systems (excepting principally Ethical Egoism) place a high premium on altruism, the sacrifice of one's self for the good of others. Postman's Park, so named because of its proximity to the General Post Office, is a monument to that altruism. Laid out in 1887, the park added 13 years later a shelter on the west side that contains dozens of engraved tablets identifying ordinary people who gave their own lives to save others: firemen, housewives, boaters, and others. Even 15 minutes of perusing the moving inscriptions will give rise to sober reflection on the nature of duty and our responsibility to one another. The plaques are moving testimonies to the bravery and decency of ordinary people. Here are a few:

John Clinton
aged 10
who drowned near
London Bridge in trying
to save a companion
younger than himself
July 16, 1894

Sarah Smith, Pantomime Artist
at the Prince's Theatre
died of terrible injuries received
when attempting in her inflammable dress
to extinguish the flames which had
enveloped her companion
January 24, 1863

Richard Farres, Labourer
was drowned in attempting to save a
poor girl who had thrown herself
into the canal at
Globe Bridge, Peckham
May 20, 1878

St. Paul's Churchyard (HENRIETTA STREET; COVENT GARDEN UNDERGROUND): This is another green oasis amidst the bustle of one of London's busiest areas. No, not that of mighty St. Paul's Cathedral. This St. Paul's is in the heart of Covent Garden, at the west end of the piazza. You'll probably see buskers resting under its portico, getting ready for a performance. During the summer the crowds and noise and activity here can make even the biggest party animal a bit crazy. There's a way almost unknown to tourists, though, to escape the hubbub.

Walk along the south side of the church on Henrietta Street. About halfway down the block you'll see a discreet sign that says "St. Paul's Churchyard." Walk through the passage and the racket and clamor melt instantly away. (If that entrance is locked, go to the end of the block, turn right on Bedford Street and try that one.) The locals come to the churchyard to escape jostling crowds and jangling telephones and to eat their lunches in peace. The churchyard is truly like the eye of a hurricane, a haven of calm and serenity in the middle of a maelstrom of noise and fury.

St. Paul's Church itself is significant. Almost a century before the great architect and church builder Sir Christopher Wren, England's most famous architect was Inigo Jones. Most of his buildings are gone now, but a few, such as the Banqueting House on Whitehall and the Queen's House in Greenwich, are among London's most wonderful. This church was designed by Inigo Jones. Nicknamed "the actor's church" because of its location in the theatre district, it contains many memorials to great actors and actresses.

STREET STUDY
The East End

If Westminster is a haven for the monied and ecclesiastical denizens of London and the City a warren of its financiers and lawyers, the East End is where the *real* people live — and have for centuries. Aside from the Tower area, you'll find few royal associations here, but the East End story may be the real story of London.

The East End has been associated with work-houses, terrible World War II bombing raids, Cockneys, criminal haunts, and even Jack the Ripper. Less than a hundred years ago nearly half the people here lived in London's most abject poverty, and 90 percent of London's Jewish community lived here. Although the sweat-shops and prostitutes have disappeared, there are still many associations with the area's heavily Jewish heritage, as well as with its earlier Christian and present Islamic orientation. The East End is a warren of twisting alleys and surprising discoveries.

Begin at Aldgate Tube Station. When you emerge from the station, the church on your right will be **St. Botolph Aldgate**. There are three St. Botolph churches in the City: at Aldgate, at Aldersgate, and at Bishopsgate. St. Botolph was the patron saint of travelers, and churches near city gates were often dedicated to him. Etched on the modern glass inner door of this church is its dedication: *For all who travel by land, air, or sea.* See the stunning stained-glass windows behind the altar in dark reds, blues, and purples.

You immediately get a feel for the East End in this church. There is much literature in the back on Christian-Jewish understanding, and the basement of the church is a relocation center for the area's homeless.

Cross busy Houndsditch outside the church. In medieval times, Jews were expected to live in this area, just outside the city walls, near the pit in which city residents tossed their dead animals. Walk north up

Duke's Place, past the Cass Foundation School. A block later, as is often the case in London, the street name changes. Now the name is Bevis Marks, a street of modern office buildings built after the horrible bombing of the Blitz. Just past Bury Street look for a gate set into the building. You've found **Bevis Marks Synagogue**, built in 1701, the oldest synagogue in Britain. Services are still conducted here each week, and the area is still heavily Jewish.

Cross Bevis Marks at St. Mary Axe Avenue, then cross Houndsditch and follow two short streets, Cutler and then Harrow, to where it dead ends into Middlesex Street. This is the site of the famous **Petticoat Lane** street market. Come on Sunday mornings for clothes, gadgets of all sorts, and some antiques. You can see spaces for booths and stalls painted on the street. At other times, things are pretty quiet, although you'll see a few fruit markets or clothing booths on side streets.

Turn left and walk north up Middlesex to where it forks to the left. On your right is the picturesquely named **Frying Pan Alley,** once the street of the metalworkers whose sign in those largely illiterate days consisted of a frying pan hung in front of the shop. The actual street is now far less interesting than its name. A better choice is to go straight ahead, up narrow **Sandy's Row.** Now you begin to feel that you've stepped back in time. Once many of the area's streets were narrow and twisting like this one, dark and closed in.

A block up Sandy's Row on the right is **Sandy's Row Synagogue.** This was built as a Christian church by the French Huguenots, Protestants who were driven out of Catholic France and worked in the weaving trade in this area. The church became a synagogue in the 1860s as the neighborhood became more Jewish.

If you walk up the street to Artillery Lane and turn into **Parliament Court**, you see on your right some tidy brick flats. They weren't always so neat. They were built in 1860 as almshouses to replace those torn down a few blocks away when New Street was built. This is typical of the East End — many interesting or attractive places, but always with a reminder of the area's grim history.

Backtrack down Sandy's Row to an even narrower street, **Artillery Passage**. This whole area was once an artillery ground set up by Henry VIII in 1537. When you come to the end of the passage on Bell Lane, you'll see across the street on your left a large homeless shelter. This 140-year-old mission still offers refuge to the area's poor. It has separate entrances for men and women.

Turn right and walk down Bell Lane until Brune Street opens to your left. About halfway down that street is the **Jewish Soup Kitchen**, set up in 1902 to feed the area's poor. The year 1902 is the year 5662 on the Jewish calendar; both dates are carved into the stone. This building kept countless East Enders alive during the bombings of World War II and continued to operate into the 1960s. It is now being restored.

At the end of Brune Street, a quick jog to the left will take you to busy Commercial Street. The large church across the street is Christ Church Spitalfields, built by French Huguenots about 1720. A block farther north, on the left-hand side of the street is **Spitalfields Market,** which has been selling food, clothing, and schlock seven days a week since 1682.

Cross the street and walk up Fournier Street, which runs along the north side of Christ Church. Take the first left (Wilkes), then the first right (Princelet). About halfway down Princelet Street is the **Spitalfields Heritage Center,** which has extensive information about the area's changing nature — Christian, then Jewish, then Muslim. An even more striking illustration of that is just a block away. At the end of Princelet, turn right on **Brick Lane**, itself the site of an excellent Sunday market. One block south, at Brick Lane and Fournier Street, is a building that sums up the area neatly.

The building was raised as a Huguenot Christian church more than 250 years ago; thereafter it was a Methodist church for a brief time, a Jewish synagogue from 1898 to 1965, and is now the chief mosque in a heavily Islamic area. Brick Lane is now lined with curry houses and bilingual street signs, acknowledging its essentially Bangladeshi character.

Following Brick Lane to its south end will take you to within a block of the Aldgate East Underground Station from which you can return, if you like, to more touristy parts of London. We prefer to stay longer, wandering through the little streets tourists never visit because nowhere in this great city is there a more colorful tapestry of evolving cultures and faiths than the East End.

IMMERSION

Honoring Religious Dissenters

A cluster of sites associated with religious reform can be found in a quarter of London where tourists seldom venture. That's too bad for the tourists, but great for you because there is none of the chaos that seems to swirl through the great cathedrals each time you begin to gain an insight into the relationships among man, mind, and Maker. That's sure to be the precise moment a tour guide elbows you out of the way and a visitor from the Republic of Macropodia steps on your foot. All chances for contemplation disappear.

John Wesley was one of the most important religious reformers of all time. Wesley was an Anglican clergyman whose powerful and emotional sermons on salvation through faith led to his banishment from English pulpits. Preaching, then, under the English sky, he brought tens of thousands to the movement called

Methodism, now one of the largest Protestant denominations. **Wesley's House, Chapel,** and the **Museum of Methodism** are located in northeast London at 47–49 City Road (OLD STREET UNDERGROUND STATION).

The house in which Wesley spent the last 12 years of his life is a simple, modest home. Wesley's books and papers are displayed here, as well as many personal items and articles of clothing. He is buried behind the house. The chapel next door, for which Wesley himself laid the cornerstone, contains the pulpit from which he preached in his last years, and a side chapel, the "Foundry Chapel," contains its original organ and pews. Lady Margaret Thatcher, former prime minister of Great Britain, was married in the main church. The museum in the crypt tells the story of Wesley's life and reform and of the Methodist Church today.

Across from the chapel is an old cemetery. Even its name suggests that it has been a burial ground for a long time, perhaps for as much as a thousand years. This is **Bunhill ("Bone-hill") Fields,** the cemetery where religious dissenters were laid to rest when Anglican churches refused to allow them into their churchyards. John Bunyan (*Pilgrim's Progress*) is buried here, as are Daniel Defoe (*Robinson Crusoe*), the mystic and artist William Blake, and hymnist Isaac Watts.

If you walk west through Bunhill Fields, you'll emerge on Bunhill Row. John Milton, the great Puritan poet, wrote *Paradise Regained* in the house at No. 125, and he died here in 1674. On the other side of the street is the Friends Burial Ground. George Fox, founder of the Society of Friends (Quakers), is buried here.

THE CROWN JEWELS

St. Paul's Cathedral: Every visitor to London knows Christopher Wren's masterwork, built after the Great Fire destroyed London in September 1666. What you may not know is that the church this one replaced, *Old* St. Paul's, was even larger than the present one, and its steeple is still the tallest ever built! But this one is quite large enough to keep you occupied for some time. It's hard to know where to start. The body of the church is simply eye-popping, although Wren's church did not include the elaborate gilding around the ceiling mosaics. That was the work of the Victorians, who believed in nothing so much as the gilding of lilies. There are monuments here to figures as diverse as Florence Nightingale, Lawrence of Arabia, and George Washington. Visit the crypt and, if you dare, pay £3 to climb to the top of the triple dome and stand outside on London's most spectacular vantage point. By all means, go to Evensong at 5 P.M. for 45 minutes of reflection, prayer, and inspiring music from the cathedral's world-renowned choir. If you're lucky, especially during the winter when there are fewer visitors, you might be invited to sit up in the choir stalls.

Two Catholic Churches: It's not nearly as old or as famous as Westminster Abbey up the street, but **Westminster Cathedral**, the chief Roman Catholic Church in Britain, is worth visiting. Completed in 1903 on land that had served as a bull-baiting ring and later as a prison, the cathedral was the final sign of a return to normalcy for the Catholic Church, abolished by Henry VIII nearly 400 years earlier. Its campanile, or bell tower, rises 273 feet, and while that's 92 feet less than St. Paul's dome, you don't have to climb to see the view; a lift will whisk you to the top. Also visit **Brompton Oratory**, a 10-minute walk west of Harrods, for a glimpse of *old* Catholicism. Although it was built in 1884, making it a fairly young church by London standards, Brompton Oratory feels *centuries* older. Almost eerily dark, there are often several Masses going on simultaneously in the various side chapels of the church. Here the altars are still against the walls and the priests conduct services with their backs to the congregation, as they did for centuries before the 1960s. There are 45 Masses a week in this church, eight of them still said in Latin.

   The Chapels of the Tower: There are countless reasons to visit the Tower, as you've discovered in even the most superficial investigation of London. Here's another one: it has two of the finest and most historic religious sites in London. The hauntingly beautiful **Chapel of St. John the Evangelist** in the White Tower is one of the finest surviving examples of a Norman chapel. The king worshiped here, and men kept vigil here the night before being knighted. Even when crowds pack the Tower in the summer, this is one place that is always cool and serene. Also within the Tower complex is the **Chapel Royal of St. Peter ad Vincula** — St. Peter in Chains. Only yards from where the headsman's block was placed, this chapel is the burial site for hundreds of former prisoners of the Tower, including three queens (Anne Boleyn, Catherine Howard, and Jane Grey) and two saints (Sir Thomas More and Bishop John Fisher) of the Catholic Church. It is open to the public for Sunday services and is part of the free tour conducted by the Yeoman Warders of the Tower.

SHERLOCK SUGGESTS . . .

London Central Mosque and Islamic Cultural Centre (PARK ROAD; MARYLEBONE UNDERGROUND): These striking buildings are at the west end of Regent's Park and include a 140-foot-tall minaret.

Jewish Museum (129–131 ALBERT STREET; CAMDEN TOWN UNDERGROUND): Dedicated to recounting the history of the Jewish faith, especially in Britain.

Bertrand Russell Memorial (RUSSELL SQUARE UNDERGROUND): A statue of the social philosopher and Nobel Prize winner stands in Red Lion Square, a few blocks south of Russell Square in Bloomsbury.

The Museum Tavern (GREAT RUSSELL STREET; TOTTENHAM COURT ROAD UNDERGROUND): Lift a pint to the father of the failed doctrine of Communism, Karl Marx. He regularly took a break here from his labors in writing *Das Kapital* in the old British Library across the street.

John Stuart Mill's House (18 KENSINGTON SQUARE; HIGH STREET KENSINGTON UNDERGROUND): This Utilitarian philosopher and follower of Bentham lived at the west end of Kensington Gardens for 14 productive years. His house is just a short walk from the Palace.

Grinling Gibbons' Carvings: Everyone is familiar with the architecture of Sir Christopher Wren. But many of his churches and many other buildings contain the artistry of one of the foremost wood carvers in the history of the world. His work on St. Paul's Cathedral is best known, but look for it elsewhere in pulpits, choir stalls, organ cases, and decorative panels. It is some of London's most beautiful artwork.

Chapter 10

Literature and Theatre

Among the things you really enjoyed in your early years of school were studying grammar and reading 400-year-old sonnets, right? Sure. And going to the dentist.

If they're honest, your high school English teachers and college English profs will admit that even they once would rather have been reading *Mad Magazine* than William Wordsworth or writing lyrics for their rock band than iambic pentameter for some teacher. But they discovered a real love of reading or writing and decided to make a career out of sharing that love. With you! And if you're reading this chapter, apparently some of their passion for English literature has rubbed off on you.

Are you ever in for a treat in London!

Nearly every literary and theatrical figure of note in the English-speaking world lived here, studied here, or worked here at one time or another. In many parts of town, you can hardly turn a corner without smacking into yet another Blue Plaque telling you that Mark Twain lived here or that *Animal Farm* was written there. A guide to literary London looks like the syllabus to English 102.

If the theatre is your literary cup of tea, you can get a great cup of tea in London. Broadway may be the theatrical center of the United States, but London's West End is the theatrical center of the world. New York has the style, but London has the substance.

Let us guide you now to the sights and sites you should not miss and several that no one else in your group will find without your aid.

THE LONDON EXPERIENCE
South of the River

The best place in London for someone interested in literature or theatre is an area that tourists seldom see much of because it is on the south, somewhat grimier, side of the Thames. Most guidebooks treat this area only as a handful of separate sights. In the next few pages, we're going to take you on a two-hour walk that will carry you through the areas that were the haunts of the likes of Chaucer, Shakespeare, and Dickens, areas that are more likely than anywhere still to be haunted by their ghosts today.

Let's start at the south end of London Bridge. You can ride the Tube to London Bridge Station or walk across the river from Monument Underground Station. Standing along the traffic-clogged street, you may have trouble conjuring up images of Dickens' London, but inhale a couple of lungsful of bus fumes and maybe you can hallucinate a suitable scene. (It probably wasn't any better in Dickens' day anyhow, except the fumes were from what the horses left behind.) Here, at the south end of London Bridge, was where Bill Sikes killed Nancy in *Oliver Twist*. We'll see a few other Dickens associations a couple of blocks away. But first turn to the large church on the west side of London Bridge Road.

This is **Southwark Cathedral**. Like many old churches, it was built in stages, but mostly it's between 600 and 700 years old. Shakespeare associations abound here. To begin with, when Will went to church, he probably came here often. We don't know precisely where he lived, but he worked nearby and, 16th-century London lacking the Tube trains and taxis of today, he probably lived close to the Globe at least part of the time. So this was most likely the church attended by *all* the actors who strode the boards down at the Globe at some time or other. We saw in the last chapter that Will also lived near Bishopsgate at one time.

A compelling piece of evidence that this was a church important to the Bard is the fact that when Will's brother Edmund Shakespeare, an actor in the company, died in 1607, he was buried here. You can find his gravestone set in the floor behind the altar. You can't miss the fine alabaster statue of a reclining Shakespeare and the nearby stained-glass window with scenes from many of his plays. If you're the scholar you try to convince your parents you are, you ought to be able to identify the plays depicted. If *we* were teaching a Shakespeare class here, we'd make that window part of our final exam.

Back out on the street, wander off to the right — that's south — along Borough High Street, a street abounding with literary associations. Many scenes from Dickens' novels took place here. He knew it well, after all. His family lived and worked here while his father languished in debtors' prison down the street.

At No. 71 Borough High Street is the **George Inn**, the last remaining galleried coaching inn in London. For hundreds of years people began or ended their London journeys at the George, staying in these very rooms. There's no telling just how long there's been an

inn here, but since Borough High Street was once an important Roman Road leading to Londinium, something close to 2000 years wouldn't be a bad guess. The present building is just a youngster, though. It was put up in 1676 after a fire damaged the previous inn. It was once much larger, but part of the building was taken down to make way for the railroad a hundred years ago.

Nevertheless, the George is in a historic neighborhood. Shakespeare's company gave performances in this courtyard. No pub in London has a better pedigree. Next door to the George, you'll find a place called Talbot Yard. For more than 600 years this was the site of the Tabard Inn, famous as the starting point for the Pilgrims in Chaucer's *Canterbury Tales*. The inn was torn down in 1875.

Continue along the east side of Borough High Street until you reach a pub called the Blue Eyed Maid at Chapel Street. Take a quick detour down the street, and you'll find **Lopex House**, one of the very few surviving Elizabethan half-timbered houses in London. Not many ordinary houses from that era are still around, what with natural aging, bombings in two world wars, assorted fires, and other disasters. Without making too big a point of it, glance through the windows and see the open-beam ceilings inside.

Continue down the street. When you reach Tabard Street, just past No. 213, look across the high street to the short street leading off to the west. That's Little Dorrit Court. Little Dorrit, one of Dickens' most loved characters, lived, was married, and died in this neighborhood. All England, including Queen Victoria, supposedly wept when the episode of the Dickens' serial appeared in which Little Dorrit died.

But you should turn left at Tabard Street. About 30 yards down on your left is what looks like a small park. It's much more than that. At the back of the lot, you'll see a worn brick wall and some rather grim-looking bars. This is all that's left of **Marshalsea Prison,** where Dickens' father was held until his debts could be paid. Dickens knew it well, and many of his novels are set near here. Even Little Dorrit lived at Marshalsea.

Now retrace your steps back toward Southwark Cathedral. Just before you get to the church, turn left onto Bedale Street and go around behind the cathedral. On the left is the short Cathedral Street and then **Clink Street.** Now you're really in an area that evokes a grimmer past. There are narrow alleyways and dark streets, although the footpads and cutpurses of an earlier day are long gone. Plenty of traces of the area's unsavory past remain, however.

You might notice here a large stone wall with an old rose window. This is all that remains of the 12th-century **Palace of the Bishop of Winchester.** For several centuries, the bishop owned all the land around here, and if you think the area looks unsavory now, you should have been here *then*! This was London's red-light district, and the good bishop owned it!

He didn't really pimp for the girls (although bishops do wear big fancy hats sometimes), but he did collect the rents from the brothels here. The working girls were known as "Winchester geese," apparently from the chattering they made in trying to attract customers. Another tactic was for a girl to run up behind a prospective . . . er, client, and grab his backside — this giving rise to the term "to goose" somebody!

No hanky-panky in this area today. The bishop is back in Winchester, the girls have moved to Camden Town, and it's a pretty quiet area now.

You'll walk down Clink Street, maybe stopping in at the old prison, but just after you pass under a railway bridge, go one block up the street to your left and turn right onto Park Street. About halfway down this street is the site of Shakespeare's original Globe Theatre. There's nothing to see now: it's fenced in so the archeologists can work, but on the wooden fence there's a large bronze plaque that's worth a quick read.

Now retrace your steps to the river and stop for a bit of refreshment at another of London's most historic pubs, the **Anchor Bankside Tavern**. There has been an inn here for centuries, and it's a sure bet that the Bard himself quaffed a pint or two in a pub on this very spot. The present building dates only from about 1770, nearly 200 years too late to have hosted Will, but whatever *was* here at the time was surely his "local," since it's just a few steps from his playhouse.

The Anchor is a wonderful place to sit on a summer night and watch the river flow by. Go late and watch them light up St. Paul's across the way for a picturebook view of London.

After you've quenched the thirst all this walking has caused, stroll a bit farther along the river, under Southwark Bridge. The street names might give you a clue to *this* area's unsavory past as well. There's Bear Gardens Alley, site of an old bear-baiting arena. And the innocently named Cardinal Cap Alley wasn't so innocent at all. It was named for the Cardinal Cap, one of the most notorious 16th-century stews — brothels.

These places were called "stews" because in those ancient days when people bathed just once a year — and then only if they needed it — some of the working girls preferred their customers to be a bit less grubby than average. So they made the men rinse off the upper layers of grime, at least, by sitting in a pot of hot water. Sometimes the bawdy bathers were joined by the girls themselves — a sort of people stew. Unless you're fond of having hot coffee spilled on your lap, you might not want to tell this story to the *stew*ardess on your flight home.

We've come to the end of our walk. Ahead of you is the reconstruction of the **Globe Theatre**, well on its way to becoming the cultural heart of Southwark. We'll leave you here to tour the theatre and hear more stories of London's literary and theatrical heritage and to reflect on just why those "Winchester Geese" thought their squawking sound would attract customers.

ON DISPLAY
The British Library Galleries

There's one place in London where you can meet scores of literary luminaries practically face to face — the galleries of the **British Library** (96 EUSTON ROAD; KING'S CROSS OR EUSTON UNDERGROUND). In these rooms you can view the original manuscripts written by the people whose names fill the index of your lit book. You'll see working copies of famous literary works, replete with cross-outs and additions; final copies ready to be sent to the printer; diaries and sketchbooks where famous people tried out their ideas. It's like looking over Beethoven's shoulder as he wrote the Fifth Symphony.

For years the British Library was part of the British Museum complex, but in 1997 and 1998 it finally moved to a new building about a half-mile away near St. Pancras Station. The new building is one of the most controversial in London. First of all, it took 14 years to complete. It ran so far over budget that the accountants haven't yet figured out how much it cost. Impatient with cost overruns and construction delays, Parliament cut its budget and reduced its size so much that on the day it opened it was already too small. And finally, thousands of people find it almost indescribably ugly.

But it's what's inside that counts. And even if the building *is* late, expensive, small, and ugly — and we don't claim to agree with any of those — the contents of its

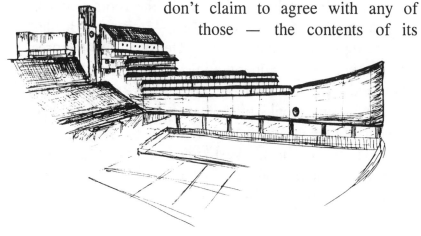

exhibition galleries are magnificent. Enter the Library through the grand portico on Euston Road and walk across the great plaza and into the building. This is not a public library, so you can't just browse among the stacks, but you *can* see the treasures of the Library. When you enter, the Exhibition Galleries will be on your left.

Wander around the room and look at all the famous literary works, written in the hand of their authors! Find the sonnet by Wordsworth. Feast your eyes on the original copy of *Alice in Wonderland*, with illustrations drawn into the manuscript by Lewis Carroll himself. Read John Milton's diary. Look at the notes Sir Walter Raleigh made for his history of the world as he sat in prison waiting for the king to order his head cut off.

Here you can see a copy of the First Folio of Shakespeare's works, as well as one of the extremely rare original signatures of the Bard and a fragment of a play believed to be written in his own hand. Want more? How about Keats, Shelley, Coleridge, Austen, Burns?

There's much more to see in the room. Musical manuscripts by Mozart, Beethoven — even the Beatles! Letters signed by monarchs from Henry VIII to the present Queen. A Gutenberg Bible. The *Magna Carta*. Thousands of illuminated manuscripts, painstakingly hand-copied by monks more than a thousand years ago. A surprise in every display case.

How good is it? Last time we took a group of American college students to the British Library, they flatly *refused* to leave for lunch!

COOL CORNERS

We're going to take you to some places associated with three of the most fascinating of all of London's countless fascinating people, and because two of these places are just a few minutes walk apart, you can slip into both these cool corners on the same afternoon. Even better, a historic pub that serves London's best pub grub is right on the way between the two. Thus fortified, it's only a 20-minute walk to the third museum.

Prince Henry's Room (17 FLEET STREET; BLACKFRIAR'S UNDERGROUND): Near Temple Bar, where the Strand turns into Fleet Street (SEE CHAPTER 11 FOR A DESCRIPTION OF THIS AREA) is an ancient Tudor half-timbered building that looks hundreds of years older than those that surround it. That's because it *is* hundreds of years older. It was built in 1608 and, without a doubt, William Shakespeare walked past it many times. In fact, it's one of the few buildings to survive from Shakespeare's day, because in 1666 more than 90 percent of the City of London burned to the ground. Somehow this building didn't.

If you enter the building, you'll get to see its nearly 400-year-old interior, and upstairs, in Prince Henry's Room, you'll find memorabilia belonging to Samuel Pepys. Pepys' diary, kept from 1660 to 1669, is one of the most interesting and revealing documents in all of English literature. He was a minor government official who as a child witnessed the execution of King Charles I in 1648, and who was present for — and wrote extensively about — the Restoration of Charles II in 1660, the Great Plague of 1665, and the Great Fire of

1666. Pepys rose steadily in government — high enough to get himself accused of treason and imprisoned in the Tower, although the king later let him go.

Few people know about Prince Henry's Room, but the chance to spend a half-hour in a building from Shakespeare's time, looking at fragments of the life of the man whose diary recounts the most dramatic decade of London's 2000-year history, should not be missed. And it's free! Seems like the hours the room is open change every time we're in London, but last time we were there it was open Monday through Saturday, 11 to 2.

Dr. Johnson's House (17 GOUGH SQUARE; CHANCERY LANE OR BLACKFRIARS UNDERGROUND): Dr. Samuel Johnson was an opinionated, curmudgeonly, sensitive literary genius. He edited the definitive edition of Shakespeare's plays, wrote the first important dictionary of the English language, covered debates in Parliament for the first true magazine in the world, and produced a literary journal that influenced dozens of English literary lights. He spent more time in coffee houses than any four people in Seattle, downed more pints of ale than your obnoxious freshman roommate, and would cheerfully have cut your philosophy professor to ribbons in an argument. He is one of the most fascinating figures in all of English literature. Boswell's biography of this powerful, larger-than-life genius makes compelling reading.

Dr. Johnson's House isn't far from Prince Henry's Room. Stroll up Fleet Street until you get to London's most famous pub, **Ye Olde Cheshire Cheese,** on the north side of the street. Stop there for lunch of bangers and mash or shepherd's pie. Be sure to go all the way downstairs and eat in what was the crypt of a monastery 600 years ago. The present building was built right after the Great Fire of 1666 and looks it, especially inside. It was supposedly the first building put up after the fire, to give the men rebuilding the city a place to eat and, perhaps, to lift a tankard or two . . . or more.

When you leave by the side entrance, turn right and you're in Gough Square. By the time you've walked a few yards into the square, the din of Fleet Street traffic disappears entirely. Make your way around the corner and you'll find a 17th-century brick building at the end of the street. This is the house where the Great Man lived from 1749 to 1759. He researched and wrote his dictionary in the garret at the top of this house, and it was here that his beloved wife died.

Johnson was a colossus who bestrode his literary era. His favor was cultivated by every literary wannabe, his criticism was more cutting and acid than the most hard-nosed professor-from-hell you ever had, and his influence was felt by everyone who wrote seriously in the English language for the next hundred years. His house is quiet and almost forgotten, but the man himself delights us — now that we're 200 years away from his rapier tongue.

From here, an easy walk up nearby Gray's Inn Road will take you to your third stop.

Dickens House (48 DOUGHTY STREET; RUSSELL SQUARE OR CHANCERY LANE UNDERGROUND): No one is more synonymous with literary London than Charles Dickens. He lived in London for most of his life, in dozens of neighborhoods in every part of town. His father was tossed into debtors' prison, and he himself worked in a grimy factory as a small boy, yet he died acclaimed the world over and his novels of the grim underside of London life stimulated countless social changes. Yet of all the many residences Dickens had in London, only one survives. This was a productive home for Dickens; he wrote *Oliver Twist* and *Nicholas Nickleby* here, as well as most of *The Pickwick Papers*.

The house is interesting in its own right for its extensive displays of Dickens' papers, but maybe the best thing about it is the fact that it's part of London's wonderful fringe-theatre scene, too. During much of the year a one-man Dickens show is performed weekly in the house's library. If you've ever wanted to meet a famous 19th-century author — and who hasn't — this is one place to almost do just that! Charles Dickens reads from his favorite works and relates the story of his life to an intimate audience numbering no more than a dozen, and sometimes only three or four. It's a memorable evening.

Street Study
Theatreland

London's West End, its theatreland equivalent of Broadway, really has two hubs. You'll undoubtedly spend lots of time in both; millions of people have spent their time, money, and virginity here and loved every minute of it. A 10-minute walk or one stop on the Piccadilly line of the Tube separates the two.

Leicester Square: At the south end of the Soho district, a warren of great restaurants and clubs, is busy Leicester Square. Everyone comes here to buy theatre tickets for half-price at the large kiosk in the center of the square — on the day of the show, cash only. Avoid the ticket touts who circulate through the crowds. Most of them are offering, at greatly inflated prices, tickets that are available at the theatre itself, and some of the tickets they sell may be counterfeit. Stick to the official half-price booth. The square is also the location of . . .

- A couple of large cinema complexes
- A substantial array of homeless people
- Numerous pairs of young lovers of every possible combination of genders walking hand-in-hand
- A big clock on the front of the Swiss House (northwest corner of the square) that puts on an amusing show every hour
- Enough late-night drunken sots that the police set up a mobile field office in a truck every night
- And much more — places that are fun, glitzy,

seedy . . . but safe. The only real crime here is a certain amount of pickpocketry, easy enough to protect yourself against if you stay watchful and sober. Go here. It's entertaining and fun.

Leicester Square is a great place to start a foray into lots of London's cultural experiences. The entire area is crowded with theatres, with *Les Miserables, Cats, Phantom, Miss Saigon,* and other blockbuster shows playing within a 10-minute walk, mostly east from the middle of the square. But 10 minutes west is Piccadilly Circus, London's version of Times Square. Soho, with its many restaurants and clubs is 10 minutes north. Chinatown, the National Gallery, the National Portrait Gallery, and Trafalgar Square are all within a five-minute walk. If you want to see how bustling — how frenetic! — London can be, Leicester Square is the place to begin. But we're supposed to be talking about more intellectual pursuits, so take a 10-minute walk east to the other West End hub, where you will find Covent Garden.

Covent Garden, a bit tamer than Soho but every bit as crowded, is a large market square where you can buy food of all types, antiques, food, crafts, food, souvenirs, food, books, food, posters, and even food. Covent Garden is just as oriented to the theatre as Soho. Numerous West End shows play within a three-minute walk of the plaza, and the Royal Opera House is here, too. **The Theatre Museum** is in Covent Garden, a must for every theatre buff, and on a more informal level, this is where you'll find London's best buskers. There's a non-stop show here — several of them, actually — all day long: magicians, dancers, contortionists, and musicians of all sorts, and they all put on great shows. Busking is a hard way to make a living, but many people do it full-time, at least during the warm weather. Spend some time talking to a busker and learn what it's like to put your talent on the line a dozen times a day, depending entirely on people's generosity and knowing that most of the people in the crowd will watch you strut your stuff and walk away without offering a tuppence for a 10- or 15-minute show. Theatre doesn't get any more real than this.

Covent Garden is just the place for an inexpensive dinner before heading out to a play or for dessert or a drink or two afterwards. If you know people in London, you'll probably meet them here, because *everybody* goes to Covent Garden.

IMMERSION
A Picnic and Play in the Park

London is a big city, packed with traffic and noise and bustle, but even in the heart of the city, it's possible to get away from the hubbub and enjoy a dose of the quiet culture you came here for. On a warm summer evening, you can't beat the Open Air Theatre in the center of Regent's Park. The theatre is nestled into a grove of trees next to Queen Mary's Rose Garden. Each summer the New Shakespeare Company presents three plays — usually two by Shakespeare and one musical — under the stars. Believe us, you can't beat spending a midsummer night watching *A Midsummer Night's*

Dream under the open sky, the way it was originally performed.

Get to the park early with a bottle of wine, some bread, and two or three interesting cheeses. Then relax in the midst of Queen Mary's Rose Garden or the broad green lawn that is just a few yards from the theatre entrance. It's a most civilized start to an evening. After you've tidied up your supper, saunter into the theatre and choose one of the delicious desserts at the concession stand. If the weather's a bit cool, you might take a glass of warm mulled wine or cider with you when you go to find your seat.

Remember, though, to bring a jacket with you; London nights are cool, even in the summer. But if you forget, you can rent a shawl or blanket at the theatre. Bring an umbrella or other rain gear if rain threatens because, in the best theatrical tradition, the performance goes on unless the weather is very bad indeed. But this is a problem only two or three times a summer.

The only downside to the theatre is that an occasional line of dialogue will be drowned out by a plane flying into Heathrow, a few miles away. But the noise is never enough to break the enchantment produced by the lovely setting, the stirring performance, and perhaps by the half bottle of wine you've consumed. It *is* a dream of a midsummer night.

What if you're spending a winter term instead of a summer term in London? Well, the Open Air Theatre is deserted and rather cold in the winter. But *fringe theatre* is just the substitute. London is packed with dozens of small theatres, some even in upstairs rooms of pubs. Here you'll find old war-horses, modern classics, Greek choruses, and bizarre experimental theatre. Some is mediocre, some is terrific, but it's inexpensive (often less than £5) and interesting. You'll see some exciting shows, and if you hit a clunker, the next one you try is sure to be better. *Time Out,* London's weekly entertainment bible, runs a comprehensive list of fringe shows in each issue.

THE CROWN JEWELS

Poets' Corner at Westminster Abbey (WEST-MINSTER UNDERGROUND): There are so many reasons to visit Westminster Abbey that we make repeated references to it throughout this book. Go! Spend as much time as you can there. Bask in the notion of being surrounded by kings and queens, scholars, statesmen, composers, and heroes in every type of human endeavor. The burial sites and memorials to the great of English literature and drama are a prime attraction. Chaucer is buried here. So is Tennyson. There are memorials to Shakespeare, to Jane Austen, to the Bronte sisters, to Laurence Olivier, to Oscar Wilde, John Milton, Charles Dickens, and dozens of other notables. Ben Jonson, Shakespeare's contemporary, is buried in another part of the Abbey — standing up to save space. (THERE'S MORE ABOUT THE ABBEY IN CHAPTER 9.)

The Globe Theatre (BANKSIDE; LONDON BRIDGE OR CANNON STREET UNDERGROUND): This isn't the same playhouse Shakespeare played in but it's an exact reproduction, opened in 1997. Will's original burned down in 1613 when a spark from a cannon being used in a play ignited the thatched roof. The only non-original details to the modern Globe are a sprinkler system in the thatch and the addition of toilets. Elizabethan audiences did what they had to do wherever they were standing at the time, but this behavior is now thought to be unsocial. Go to a play at the Globe and by all means buy 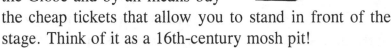 the cheap tickets that allow you to stand in front of the stage. Think of it as a 16th-century mosh pit!

SHERLOCK SUGGESTS . . .

Cheyne Walk (CHELSEA; SLOANE SQUARE UNDERGROUND): This neighborhood has housed dozens of great poets, novelists, artists, and playwrights. Some, like Oscar Wilde, are still popular, but the stars of others have faded. (Read any Dante Gabriel Rossetti lately?) Chelsea is a relatively quiet residential neighborhood near the Thames. It may have lost the rural charm that led Henry VIII to build a summer house here, but 300 years later it was *the* place to live for the British *literati*.

The Sherlock Holmes Museum (BAKER STREET; BAKER STREET UNDERGROUND): What could be more appropriate in this category than a visit to a building that calls itself 221B Baker Street. It isn't really; it's at 208. No. 221 would be where the Abbey National Bank is located, a bit up the street. But so what! If you're a fan of the Holmes tales, you'll find this museum very well done and true to the stories. It also provides a wonderful glimpse into the lodgings and lives of Victorian Londoners.

Sherlock Holmes Pub (NORTHUMBERLAND AVENUE; CHARING CROSS UNDERGROUND): There's another nice reproduction of Holmes' sitting room next to the second-floor restaurant of this pub.

St. Margaret's Church (WESTMINSTER UNDERGROUND): This church, adjacent to Westminster Abbey, is where John Milton was married. There is a memorial to him at the west end of the church.

Chapter 11

Communication

No city in the world but New York can rival London as a place to study communication. Whether you are studying journalism, broadcasting, film, interpersonal communication, organizational communication, media management, or anything else that involves creating text, sound, or visuals for others to read, watch, or listen to (have we covered the bases?), then London is optimal.

Your study enhancement can begin with a Sunday trip to Speakers' Corner in Hyde Park. Other wonderful options are going through the Museum of the Moving Image, attending the filming of a British Broadcasting Corporation (BBC) television production, or walking along Fleet Street, once the hub of British journalism.

THE LONDON EXPERIENCE
Politics, Society, and Salvation at Speakers' Corner

After taking the Underground to Marble Arch Station, you find yourself in a perplexing maze of tunnels that emerge at different locations around **Marble Arch** itself, a grandiose 19th-century archway that, since it leads nowhere in particular, is in effect nothing more than a toweringly eye-catching traffic divider. Actually Marble Arch stood in front of Buckingham Palace from 1828 until 1851, when the palace was re-designed and the arch no longer fit into the scheme.

Invariably, in exiting the Underground, you choose the wrong tunnel, come up by the arch itself, and have to re-enter the concrete rabbit warren to try your luck again. That's okay. We always do and we've been there many times. Tunnel roulette is the first installment of the fun that a trip to **Speakers' Corner** provides.

If you arrive when late morning is giving way to midday, then you'll find a few hundred people milling about, listening to a half-dozen to a dozen speakers. What are they speaking about? Well, two or three are likely to be religious proselytizers of one stripe or the other trying to salvage lost souls — including yours. Inevitably there's an aging Marxist who hasn't given up on the notion of a worker's paradise, there's someone in favor of more women's rights, someone in favor of fewer women's rights, someone who wants to expel all the immigrants, and someone who thinks immigrants are the spice in the social stew. You can usually count on a speaker railing against the Great Satan — the United States — and its president.

Spending an hour listening to the fervid, the fanatic, and frequently the loony may not sound like the best way to spend part of a Sunday in London. But believe us — it is! It's not just because of the speakers. To be sure, a few of them have some good points to make and one or two are likely to be laughably off their rockers, but the most mirthful, as well as thought-provoking, moments come from the verbal sparring between a speaker and the audience. People in the crowd challenge the speakers, often to the point of taunting them.

In fact, every time we've ever been, a supremely sarcastic, bitingly snippy, and outrageously funny heckler has been a thorn in the side of whichever speaker he's tormenting at the moment. This rotund little middle-aged man, whose sparse thatch of sandy red hair is typically hidden under a ballcap, would have his own late-night talk show in the United States. While he usually brings a large measure of grief to the speaker he's heckling, his snappy retorts often lead to a doubling or tripling of the assembled crowd. Could he secretly be in the pay of the British Tourist Au-  thority? This man must be depicted in 10,000 photo albums in the United States alone. He skewers the liberals over their politics, pokes fun at the pious preachers, and generally gores any speaker whose ideas deviate from his own. Therein lies the joy of Speakers' Corner — that highly charged give and take.

The surprising thing is how rarely there's any trouble, given the oft-provocative topics and hurled insults. Speakers' Corner, the ultimate representation of freedom of speech, could exist in few countries. Gunplay would be the likely outcome of an attempt to replicate Speakers' Corner in an American city. But in Britain, most people just smile and take it all in. A few get hot under the collar, but the war of words hardly ever escalates to any physical confrontation. Besides, inevitably a police officer or two will be patrolling the place and show up just in the nick of time to squelch any trouble.

The last time one of us was at Speakers' Corner, the exceptional occurred. A self-righteous Aussie preacher lost his cool under the relentless heckling of the wit described in the previous paragraphs. Suddenly the Aussie snapped, leapt off his crate, and, wielding his rather formidable umbrella like a sword, gave chase to the astonished heckler. The heckler couldn't escape quickly enough through the thick crowd. The preacher, a sinewy man of about 60, tackled the diminutive heckler and began to pummel him with the metal spike of the umbrella. Bystanders pulled the crazed man of God off his victim, who was bleeding from a couple of minor facial wounds. The police were on the spot in a jiffy and began to try to sort out the mess. Remember that such scuffles are the exception, not the rule. It's the only confrontation like that we've ever seen. The closest that you're likely to come to physical misadventure at Speakers' Corner is being accidentally elbowed or stepped on by the person beside you, unless you laugh so hard that you split your sides.

The crowd is composed mostly of tourists from the world over, but Londoners show up too. After all, it's free entertainment.

The best way to size up Speakers' Corner is to go about 11:30 A.M. and spend 45 minutes roaming from speaker to speaker, getting a flavor of each's rhetoric. Then wander west along the northern edge of Hyde Park until you come to the Lancaster Gate area of Bayswater Road. Leave the park and stroll west on the park side of **Bayswater Road,** which will be lined with the bounty of artists — watercolors, paintings, prints, drawings, collages — and a hodgepodge of other things such as miniature pub signs and cleverly designed clocks. Even if you aren't inclined to buy anything, looking at the art on Bayswater Road is another of the joys of a Sunday in London.

After you've put away a plate of roast and potatoes or shepherd's pie from the Swan pub or another Bayswater Road eatery, walk back to Speakers' Corner, where things ought to be peaking. The crowd has swelled to 400 or so, and there are a dozen or more speakers ranting from atop their plastic crates. Another 30 to 45 minutes of rabble-rousers ought to aid your digestive process.

Most of you will enjoy Speakers' Corner so much that you'll want to come back. A few of you might screw up your courage and give a shot at speaking. Some of our students have — acquitting themselves well and etching into the memories of our group members one of their most vivid London images.

ON DISPLAY
Museum of the Moving Image

You'll find the **Museum of the Moving Image** (MOMI) near the Waterloo Bridge (WATERLOO UNDERGROUND) on the south bank of the Thames. MOMI, which opened in 1988, isn't your garden-variety museum. You can't go through MOMI on intellectual cruise control because the exhibits grab you (literally, sometimes) and involve you in the story of the evolution of film and television. If you go with others from your group, it's a safe bet that one or more of you is going to be accosted, in a non-threatening way, by some figure from a bygone era who pulls you into the time warp too. We've auditioned for a shoot-em-up Hollywood western, danced the Charleston, and belted out a rendition of *A Bicycle Built for Two*.

Few exhibits at MOMI are static. You experience the past and confront the present: daguerreotypes, lantern slides, Hollywood's founding, Mary Pickford, Charlie Chaplin, the development of BBC television, *Dr. Who*, Jim Henson. All come alive at MOMI. (Figuratively, at least. We're sorry to report that Mary, Charlie, Jim, *et al.* are still dead.) Not only is MOMI a *fun* museum for people of all ages, but the extensiveness of its holdings are enough to satisfy the purest purist.

COOL CORNERS OF LONDON
The BBC TV Studios

When drawing up your list of places to go in London, you probably didn't consider the BBC television studios. For communication students, the BBC studios are a cathedral of culture. You should go there to watch the making of a program. Tickets are surprisingly easy to get, particularly if you arrange for them well in advance by contacting the BBC Television ticket unit.

We have arranged for our students to go to the filming of sitcoms *Chalk* and *Bloomin' Marvellous*. The address and phone number of the BBC ticket unit were available at the BBC World Wide Web site *(http://www.bbc.co.uk)*. A telephone call and a fax later, we had our reservations. To be certain, the most famous, top-rated programs aren't as likely to be available, but something usually is if you are flexible. If you don't want to bother arranging anything in advance, just try contacting the ticket unit after you arrive. You'll almost certainly get the chance to see something.

In fact, everything about this is easy. The Central

Line of the Underground takes you to the White City stop, from which it's a five-minute walk to the BBC Television Centre. As you come out of the Tube station, you can see the building in your field of view and to the left. The large, ungainly building would look perfectly at home among the concrete urban sprawl of Eastern Europe, but this bad architecture can't be blamed on Socialist chic.

Once you've cleared security and been ushered into the studio, the fun begins. If you've never been to the taping of a television show, you can count on the experience being quite different from what you'd imagine — no matter how vivid your imagination. Someone may warm up the audience by describing the series concept and telling you what to expect over the course of the evening. But soon, the camera crews are out, the director is . . . well, directing. The actors are in their places, and the show begins.

A scene is performed, and you think it's great. The director, however, doesn't, so they take it from the top. Again and again. Apparently the directors' union requires that each scene be done at least four times, no matter how perfectly the actors execute it or how strongly the audience responds.

Finally, the director is happy with the last scene, and *it's a wrap!*

The BBC isn't the only game in town as far as television program making, so there are other productions to be seen. The ITV network, which broadcasts the commercial channel 3, consists of regional franchises. Two broadcasters have ITV franchises for London, one for weekdays and the other for weekends. The weekday broadcaster, Carlton, and the weekend broadcaster, London Weekend Television, both make some shows. Many series are made by independents, such as Thames Television, the heavyweight in that category. The other two commercial terrestrial channels, 4 and 5, are also headquartered in London, as are numerous channels that are broadcast via satellite and cable.

STREET STUDY
The Ghosts of Fleet Street

Journalism students should walk down Fleet Street and try to imagine that for two centuries this was the heart of British newspaperdom and even before that was the heart of the printing industry. The daily newspapers have relocated to the South Bank of the Thames, but there are still clues to the journalistic heritage of Fleet Street.

Fleet Street begins where the Strand ends at **Temple Bar,** a column topped by a rather imposing Griffin (no relation to the author) that marks the entrance to the City of London. As you walk along Fleet Street, look for the bust of Lord Northcliffe on the front of St. Dunstan in the West Church. Lord Northcliffe, Alfred Harmsworth, was a 19th-century newspaper baron whose empire included *The Daily Mail* and *The Daily Mirror.*

175

The stately former headquarters of *The Daily Telegraph* is No. 135. You should also take note of the former **Daily Express Building** (Nos. 121–128), a 1931 black-glass behemoth that stirs the blood of modern-architecture enthusiasts but leaves traditionalists cold. Years of emptiness and neglect are taking their toll. A journalistic pulse still emanates from No. 85, the head-quarters of Reuters news agency and the Press Association. An exhibit in the crypt of **St. Bride's Church** (built by . . . who else? Christopher Wren) pays tribute to the journalistic heritage of Fleet Street. (THERE'S MORE ABOUT ST. BRIDE'S IN CHAPTER 8.)

If you try hard, you can conjure up the competitive newspaper world that was Fleet Street, but this is no street museum. Rather, it pulsates with the noises of commerce. Step off the street to enter another time. The alley at No. 145 leads to the **Cheshire Cheese,** a pub that was *rebuilt* in 1667 after the Great Fire of London, and whose clientele included Dr. Samuel Johnson, the 18th-century lexicographer whose house is nearby on Gough Square. Regardless of whether you encounter the ghosts of wordsmiths, you can have a tasty yet inexpensive lunch and a pint of Britain's best. Journalists and other writers were also *habitues* of El Vino's wine bar (No. 47) and Ye Olde Cock Tavern (No. 22). Other popular pubs for journalists were the Old Bell Inn, the Punch Tavern, and the Wig and Pen Club. Journalists are a drunken lot!

IMMERSION
Sampling the Media

Even if you don't go out to watch the recording of a British television program, you ought to watch the telly the odd hour here and there while resting between adventures. For one thing, as a communication student, you may be talking about British TV in your classes and your learning will be greatly enhanced by drawing your own conclusions. For another, watching TV can be a fun change of pace. You'll find similarities and differences between British television and television at home. The Brits, for example, are ga-ga over a few prime-time soap operas and series about police or other crime-solvers. If, however, you find yourself spending more than three hours *a week* watching TV while in London — GET OFF YOUR LAZY BUTT, YOU COUCH POTATO, AND LIVE A LITTLE. YOU'RE IN LONDON, FOR GOSH SAKES!

In the same vein, but much easier to fit into your schedule, would be sampling British newspapers, which run the gamut from outstanding, serious journalistic endeavors to tabloids that thrive on sex, sleaze, and scandal. The British newspaper scene is the most competitive in Europe and among the most competitive worldwide. Nine nationally distributed general-interest dailies are published in London, so there's something for everybody. Three are mass-appeal tabloids — *The Sun, The Daily Mirror,* and *The Star.* Collectively known as the "redtops" because their nameplates are set against a red background, these papers serve up a daily helping of sensational news and cheesecake photos. *The Sun* introduced into British popular culture the Page 3 Girl — a topless or otherwise scantily clad young woman displayed poster-like on page 3 — and the other two redtops play the skin game as well. Two tamer tabloids, *The Daily Mail* and *The Express*, put more emphasis on news than flesh but never ignore a juicy scandal. London also offers four highly respected, quality newspapers, *The Times, The Guardian, The Daily Telegraph,* and *The Independent.* Any communication student — really, any student — should pick up a British paper regularly because not only do they provide for interesting comparisons of journalistic approach, but they also provide insight into British culture. Don't keep reading the same one. Try them all.

Going to a British film would provide another change of pace from your hectic study/touring schedule. *Finding* a British film is your first challenge. Although Hollywood films dominate the cinemas, there will invariably be a few British films to choose from. When in doubt, head to **Leicester Square,** on or near which are a number of cineplexes, including the Odeon Leicester Square, the Odeon West End, the Warner West End, the Empire, and the MGM Swiss Centre. A number of contemporary British filmmakers have garnered international acclaim in recent years, including Mike Leigh (*Secrets and Lies*), Ismail Merchant and James Ivory (*Howard's End*), Kenneth Branagh (*Much Ado About Nothing*), Danny Boyle (*Trainspotting*), and Mike Newell (*Four Weddings and a Funeral*). If you are interested in classics, try the **National Film Theatre** on the South Bank near Waterloo Bridge.

CROWN JEWELS

The Houses of Parliament (PARLIAMENT SQUARE; WESTMINSTER UNDERGROUND): Students interested in political communication, debating, or the circulation of hot air should attend a session of Parliament. You can queue up outside Parliament in the afternoon for a wait that will likely be anywhere from a half-hour to two hours. Once inside, you can observe the House of Commons, the House of Lords, or both. Optimally, go for the Prime Minister's Question Time, when the prime minister usually provides prickly responses to the poisoned arrows of rowdy opposition party members. This is the war of words at its finest. Insults fly and decorum dissipates. Granted, the Taiwanese parliament, where fistfights occasionally break out, is more fractious, but the figurative blood shed here provides ample entertainment. If you go for a regular session, the rhetoric is likely to be less vituperative. In the House of Lords, in fact, you may be startled by empty seats and snoozing geezers. Government in action! (THERE'S MORE ABOUT PARLIAMENT IN CHAPTER 12.)

The British Library (EUSTON ROAD; KING'S CROSS/ST. PANCRAS UNDERGROUND): The British Library moved in 1997 from the ground floor of the British Museum to a grand new facility on Euston Road near St. Pancras Station. Communication students shouldn't miss the two original copies of the 13th-century *Magna Carta* and books by early printers Wyken de Worde, William Caxton, and Johannes Gutenberg, whose renowned Bible can be seen. (THERE'S MORE ABOUT THE BRITISH LIBRARY IN CHAPTER 10.)

SHERLOCK SUGGESTS . . .

BBC Experience (PORTLAND PLACE; OXFORD CIRCUS 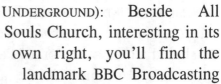 UNDERGROUND): Beside All Souls Church, interesting in its own right, you'll find the landmark BBC Broadcasting House, home to BBC Radio since 1932. The interactive and multi-media BBC Experience slickly tells the story of BBC radio and tele-vision through the ages. The shop is a good place to find BBC doodads or BBC audio-tapes and videotapes.

Bush House (THE STRAND; TEMPLE UNDERGROUND): The headquarters of the BBC World Service is at Bush House. Adjacent is a small shop where you can buy BBC items.

Science Museum (EXHIBITION ROAD; SOUTH KENSINGTON UNDERGROUND): Don't be fooled by the title of this South Kensington museum. Galleries dedicated to the history of printing, photography, and cinematogra-phy make the Science Museum a worthwhile rainy-day destination for communication students. The sadly ne-glected telecommunication gallery desperately needs a re-do. (THERE'S MORE ABOUT THE SCIENCE MUSEUM IN CHAPTER 15.)

Reuter Memorial (OFF THREADNEEDLE STREET;

BANK UNDERGROUND): Baron Paul Julius von Reuter, who founded the news agency that bears his name, is commemorated with a memorial behind the Royal Exchange.

Dr. Johnson's House (17 GOUGH SQUARE; BLACKFRIARS OR CHANCERY LANE UNDERGROUND): The noted lexicographer lived here from 1749 to 1759. You can see first editions of Dr. Johnson's dictionary, which he worked on while living in this house. (THERE'S MORE ABOUT DR. JOHNSON'S HOUSE IN CHAPTER 10.)

Marconi's Residence (71 HEREFORD ROAD; BAYSWATER UNDERGROUND): Guglielmo Marconi, whose experiments with wireless telegraphy gave rise to the development of radio, lived here.

British Telecom Tower (CLEVELAND STREET; GOODGE STREET UNDERGROUND): You'll notice this 619-foot tower, London's tallest building when it was completed in the mid-1960s, so you may as well know what it is.

Baird's Laboratory (22 FRITH STREET; TOTTENHAM COURT ROAD UNDERGROUND): Television pioneer John Logie Baird demonstrated TV for the first time in 1926 in an attic room at this Soho address.

Alexandra Palace (HARINGEY; EAST FINCHLEY UNDERGROUND): This palace is where the BBC made the first live television broadcast in 1936. The palace, rebuilt after a 1980 fire, stands amid a 480-acre park in the borough of Haringey.

National Film Theatre (SOUTH BANK ARTS CENTRE; WATERLOO UNDERGROUND): The National Film Theatre, on the South Bank just east of Waterloo Bridge, has two movie theatres where you can find all sorts of special film screenings.

Chapter 12

Political Science, Criminal Justice, and Law

London, the seat of Britain's government and home to its monarch, has much of interest to the student of political science. Parliament beckons, as do Buckingham Palace, Kensington Palace, and a host of other places where blood runs blue. That great charter of English liberties, the *Magna Carta*, laid the groundwork for a system of political and civil liberties that has been eight centuries in the making. Those pursuing criminal justice will want to probe deeper than the touristic image of the "bobby" with his distinctive headgear and learn how the Metropolitan Police in London deal with contemporary problems that plague any metropolis, much less a world capital. The Inns of Court are just one facet of the legal system that law students will want to explore.

THE LONDON EXPERIENCE
A Session of Parliament

Going to a session of **Parliament** (PARLIAMENT SQUARE; WESTMINSTER UNDERGROUND) is a great way to get insight into the British political system, and it has the added advantage of being one of the easiest ways to get into the building to appreciate its design. Otherwise, you'd have to arrange a tour through a member of Parliament, and you probably don't have the name of one in your Rolodex. Come to think of it, you probably don't even have a Rolodex yet.

When Parliament is in session, you can queue up outside for admission and wait as the line inches forward. The House of Commons meets at 2:30 P.M. Monday through Thursday and at 9:30 A.M. Friday. If you're lucky, the line will be short and you'll be inside in a jiffy. A wait of an hour isn't uncommon in the summertime, but the magnificent views of St. Margaret's Church, Westminster Abbey, and Parliament itself, combined with the fumes of taxis whizzing by, are likely to leave you giddy. Here's a tip: Parliament usually meets until late in the evening, so if you don't want to wait, go after 6 P.M. You can usually get in at once. Inside, you'll be directed to the House of Commons.

From your vantage point in the Visitors' Galleries, the government party MPs (members of Parliament) will be seated on the left and the opposition party MPs will be on the right.

What you experience depends very much on what the issues of the day are. When we were last there, the debate was so perfunctory that staying awake — no, let's make that conscious — was a monumental challenge. The head of one of the co-authors jerked up and down as if he were a marionette. Go anyway. The chance to observe government in action and to admire the beautiful surroundings more than makes up for the risk of heavy eyelids.

The House of Commons, model of democratic debate for the world, is known as the Mother of Parliaments. It also is known for fractious bickering between the parties, with MPs hurling barbs and insults back and forth. Your chances of observing that sort of verbal sparring would be increased if you go for what's known as the Prime Minister's Question Time. The prime minister takes questions from fellow members of Parliament on Tuesdays and Thursdays at 3:15 P.M. As the opposition assails the policies of the party in power, sparks usually fly. A veneer of civility *(The Honorable Member across the aisle . . .)* fails to disguise the sneering insults *(. . . is a feeble-minded arse).*

After you've had a chance to observe democracy

in action in the House of Commons — and to appreciate the magnificent room and its trappings of power — cross over to the House of Lords if it is also in session. The House of Lords typically meets at 2:30 P.M. on Monday through Wednesday, at 3 P.M. on Thursday, and 11 A.M. on Friday. The Lords may be less dynamic than the Commons. When we last went, catnaps weren't confined to the Strangers' Gallery. Half of the Lords — and only a handful were there — were snoozing as well.

Look for the throne, where the Queen sits when she formally opens a session of Parliament. She won't be there while you are in the Strangers' Gallery, nor should anyone else be there, unless there's been a *coup d'etat*. Also, take note of the Woolsack, which looks like an oversized ottoman. This is where the symbol of the sovereign's authority, the mace, is placed when the Lords are meeting.

ON DISPLAY
The National Portrait Gallery

Putting a face with the names of the mighty politicians who have changed the course of British and world history is gratifying. **The National Portrait Gallery** (ST. MARTIN'S PLACE; CHARING CROSS UNDERGROUND) overwhelms the non-selective visitor, but you can have a pleasant experience by focusing on the portraits of those who really interest you. Students of political science will find much of note. Kings, queens, prime ministers, and politicians achieve a measure of immortality on the walls. Among the offerings: portraits of current Royal Family members, monarchs through the ages, Oliver

Cromwell, Benjamin Disraeli, William Gladstone, Winston Churchill, and Margaret Thatcher. (THERE'S MORE ABOUT THE NATIONAL PORTRAIT GALLERY IN CHAPTER 15.)

COOL CORNERS

Kensington Palace (KENSINGTON GARDENS; HIGH STREET KENSINGTON UNDERGROUND): Royalty reside here, so this is your chance to imagine what life would be like if your mom and pop were monarchs.

Kensington Palace is hardly a secret, but few visitors to London have it in their list of Top 10 must sees. They should, because an outing here (in the old-fashioned sense) makes for a great afternoon.

The palace, which dates to the early 17th century, was bought by King William III in 1689 and renovated by architect Christopher Wren, who designed so many buildings in or around London that one wonders if he represents an early success with human cloning.

Princess Margaret lives here, and various other royals make this their home as well. Prince Charles and Princess Diana resided here before the breakup of their marriage, and Diana continued living in Kensington Palace afterward. Your memory may flicker with an image of a sea of flowers placed in front of the gate after Princess Diana's death in 1997.

Jewel Tower (OLD PALACE YARD; WESTMINSTER UNDERGROUND): The Jewel Tower is the overlooked gem (sorry, couldn't resist) in the Parliament Square area. Visitors to London are so captivated by Parliament and Westminster Abbey that they typically fail to notice this 14th-century tower. You'd think a six-century-old building whose story is woven into the history of the country would be a major tourist attraction, but the Jewel Tower is probably less visited than the Boots Pharmacy across from Big Ben. Part of the original Palace of Westminster, this tower became a storehouse for the Crown Jewels and later was used to store parliamentary records. The exhibit takes you through the history of Parliament.

The Banqueting House (WHITEHALL; CHARING CROSS OR WESTMINSTER UNDERGROUND): You'd never guess the historical significance of this place if you were just judging by its name or gazing at the elegant but restrained facade from the street. When Whitehall Palace was badly damaged in a fire, James I had architect Inigo Jones begin work on a new palace on the same site. Only the Banqueting House was completed, in 1622. The main hall, with its ceiling paintings designed by Peter Paul Rubens, is stunning. Charles I, who commissioned the ceiling work, must have been pleased with the results. He not only paid Rubens, but he also knighted him for good measure. Charles I was presumably much less pleased with his last visit to the Banqueting House. After the Crown lost its war against Oliver Cromwell and the Parliamentarians in 1649, Charles was led through a window to a scaffold in front of the building and executed. The beauty and serenity of the

Banqueting House, overlooked by most visitors and therefore remarkably peaceful, belies its connection to one of the most tumultuous moments in British history.

STREET STUDY
Legal London

London often seems like a city straddling a fault line in time. Old buildings stand adjacent to modern ones, traditions compete with trends. It almost seems as if the unwinding of history is marred by kinks. To a certain extent, this is true of many places, but it is truer of London than of most. Nowhere are these contrasts more evident than where Westminster gives way and the City of London begins. An exploration of legal London brings one face to facade with many of these contrasts. The heart of legal London beats at the four Inns of Court and the Royal Courts of Justice. The **Inns of Court** — Middle Temple, Inner Temple, Gray's Inn, and Lincoln's Inn — have served as headquarters for lawyers and law students since the 14th century. English barristers must belong to one of the four Inns of Court. Many have their offices, referred to as chambers, at the inns. The Temple name predates the lawyers. The Temple area was a seat of the Order of the Knights Templar, which was dissolved early in the 14th century by Pope Clement V.

Begin your exploration by taking the Tube to Temple Station and walking along Victoria Embankment until you come to Middle Temple Gateway, a wonderful 17th-century arch leading to Middle Temple Lane.

As you walk north on Middle Temple Lane,

you'll come to the Middle Temple Hall, on the left. If you want to visit Middle Temple Hall to see its Elizabethan great hall, which is usually closed, you'd need to make a special arrangement. Calming quiet defines the entire Temple area, stirring one's reflective senses.

A passageway to the right leads to the Inner Temple. The verdant Inner Temple Gardens extend a green arm toward the Thames. On the left is the Inner Temple Hall and Library, built in the 1950s to replace their predecessors, which were destroyed in World War II. As you wend your way around them, you will come to a courtyard that contains **Temple Church.** The 12th-century circular nave, called the Round, is one of the few remaining round churches in England. The floor contains effigies of nine Knights Templar. If the timing deities are with you, you may be lucky enough to catch a midday concert.

After you've seen the church, meander west (don't you wish you'd brought your Scout compass with you?) back in the general vicinity of Middle Temple Lane. You'll want to see the lovely Middle Temple Gardens. If the gate isn't locked, here would be the perfect spot for a pause. Even if it isn't open, you can rest your body while feasting your eyes at **Fountain Court,** to the north of the garden, up a flight of steps. As you walk toward Fountain Court, peruse the windows in the lawyer's digs to the left. You are likely to espy a barrister's powdered wig or two on dummies' heads (no *double entendre* intended). The 17th-century fountain beckons law students, lawyers, and visitors alike with its graceful spray of water and contemplation.

Once you've had your fill from this oasis, take the passageway to the north, which leads to the Strand. When you emerge onto the sidewalk of the Strand, your gaze will be caught by the imposing neo-Gothic facade of the **Royal Courts of Justice,** which looks somewhat like a castle plopped down in the City. Cross over for a closer look. If you want to sit in on a trial, you may do so, but you won't get in with a camera, and there are no facilities for storing it.

If you continue east on the Strand past the Royal Courts of Justice, you'll come to Chancery Lane. Turn left onto Chancery and walk for a few minutes until you come to a 16th-century brick gatehouse on your left. Look for the coat of arms of Henry VIII above the oak doors. The gateway will lead you to New Square, part of Lincoln's Inn, another of the Inns of Court. You should see the Chapel, which is to your right after you pass through the gatehouse. On the southeast corner of the square, an archway leads to Carey Street. Position yourself near the archway about 10 minutes before the start of an hour. Then you have a good chance of seeing some wig-toting or wig-wearing barrister heading to the Royal Courts of Justice for a session. The legal book-shops that open onto the archway add to the picturesque setting.

Other points of interest in the Lincoln's Inn area are the Old Hall and the New Hall and library. The library, which dates to 1497, is the oldest in London and contains a vast collection of law books. The Lincoln's Inn area is lovely, with bursts of color from flower beds set off by the green of perfectly manicured lawns that contrast with the stone and brick of buildings. Another gateway leads to Lincoln's Inn Fields, a large square around which stand many fine houses, including that of the architect Sir John Soane.

Just north of Lincoln's Inn lies High Holborn, a major thoroughfare. Cross to the north side of the street and turn right. By this point you probably need a break. Walk along High Holborn a few minutes until you reach the **Cittie of York** pub, one of London's finest watering holes. What awaits are three rooms with distinctly different personalities: a traditional cozy room; a huge, high-ceilinged room with immense wine barrels overhead along one wall; and a crypt. Three pubs in one — how can you beat that! The clientele is mostly of the dark-suit, white-shirt type, along with a smattering of equally spiffy businesswomen. Cittie of York is arguably one of the 10 coolest pubs in London, and the food in the crypt isn't half-bad.

Continue your exploration by walking farther east along High Holborn. Across from the intersection with Gray's Inn Road, you'll see a lovely, expansive timber-framed building. That's the 16th-century **Staple Inn,** one of the oldest timber-framed buildings remaining in London. Originally a hostel for wool staplers, Staple Inn later became an Inn of Chancery, which it remained until 1884. The nine Inns of Chancery had a standing in the legal profession a notch below the Inns of Court.

Turn left onto Gray's Inn Road, where a little ways up you'll find Gray's Inn Square and Gray's Inn Gardens. This is the final Inn of Court. Enjoy the gardens, whose design is credited to Francis Bacon, who was treasurer of the Inn and resided there the last half-century of his life. After getting your fill of Gray's Inn, retrace your steps along Gray's Inn Road to High Holborn.

Walk farther east along Holborn, past Holborn Circus. The street name changes to Holborn Viaduct. Look for the **Central Criminal Court,** nicknamed the Old Bailey for the street that runs along one side. It will be on your right just after you pass St. Sepulchre's Church on the left. Atop the Central Criminal Court is a bronze statue of justice, replete with sword and scales. Nearby is the site of Newgate Prison, outside of which criminals were executed from 1783 to 1868, and where executions continued inside until 1901. The prison was torn down the next year.

IMMERSION

In the Footsteps of Revolutionaries

Political dissidents have always flocked to London, and chasing their shadows can make for an interesting afternoon or two.

Karl Marx (1818–1883), whose political and economic ideas gave birth to Communism, moved to England in 1849. Marx and his family lived from 1851–1856 in a cramped apartment at 28 Dean Street, now marked by a blue plaque. In the former Reading Room of the British Library on Great Russell Street, Marx wrote much of *Das Kapital* (FOR EITHER SITE, USE TOTTENHAM COURT ROAD UNDERGROUND). Marx's grave is in Highgate Cemetery (HIGHGATE UNDERGROUND). Also of interest may be the Marx Memorial Library, 37A Clerkenwell Green (FARRINGDON UNDERGROUND).

V. I. Lenin (1870–1924), whose revolutionary fervor sparked the overthrow of Imperial Russia and the formation of the Soviet Union, lived in a house in Holford Square near King's Cross in 1902. A plaque behind the Royal Scott Hotel, 100 King's Cross Road (FOR EITHER SITE, USE KING'S CROSS/ST. PANCRAS UNDERGROUND), indicates that Lenin stayed in a house nearby on Percy Circus in 1905. In the Marx Memorial Library in Clerkenwell (SEE MARX ENTRY ABOVE), Lenin edited *Iskra* in 1902 and 1903.

The Italian patriot **Giuseppe Mazzini** (1803–1872) lived in London during his exile. Mazzini lived at 183 Gower Street (EUSTON SQUARE UNDERGROUND) in Bloomsbury from 1837, when he arrived in London, until 1840. A blue plaque marks the address. Another blue plaque, at 10 Laystall Street (CHANCERY LANE UNDERGROUND), indicates the site where Mazzini founded the Garibaldi and Mazzini Operatives' Society for Italian workers. At Hatton Garden (CHANCERY LANE OR FARRINGDON UNDERGROUND), in London's "Little Italy," Mazzini lived at No. 5, and a tablet here with Mazzini's portrait pays tribute to him.

Mahatma Gandhi (1869–1948), the Indian patriot, is commemorated with a statue in Tavistock Square in Bloomsbury (EUSTON OR RUSSELL SQUARE UNDERGROUND).

Sun Yat Sen, a Chinese exile who returned home to lead the Kuomintang revolt against the Ch'ing Dynasty, lived at 4 Gray's Inn Place (CHANCERY LANE UNDERGROUND) in the 1890s. A plaque commemorates Sun.

THE CROWN JEWELS

The Crown Jewels (TOWER OF LONDON; TOWER HILL UNDERGROUND): Would you really expect us to put them in any other category? Go, gawk, reflect. The monarchy's power has run the gamut from near absolute to largely ceremonial. Glittering crowns and bejeweled maces evoke the images of long-dead kings and queens as well as the current monarch.

Buckingham Palace (GREEN PARK; ST. JAMES PARK, OR VICTORIA UNDERGROUND): Parts of Buckingham Palace have been toured by the public since 1993 for two months each summer to raise funds for the repair of Windsor Castle, extensively damaged in a 1992 fire, but the tours were not planned to be offered permanently. So now, unless you get a surprise invitation to tea with the Queen, the closest you'll come is likely to be the Changing of the Guard ceremony, which is worth attending, although you really need to watch your wallet or purse because pickpockets work this crowd despite the heavy police presence. Don't forget — the Palace is about more than pomp and pageantry. The monarch occupies an important, albeit largely symbolic, role in British politics.

SHERLOCK SUGGESTS . . .

Magna Carta (BRITISH LIBRARY, 96 EUSTON ROAD; KING'S CROSS/ST. PANCRAS UNDERGROUND): The British Library has two of the existing four "exemplifications" of this 1215 charter of English liberties, both with the seal of King John. (THERE'S MORE ABOUT THE BRITISH LIBRARY IN CHAPTERS 10 AND 11.)

10 Downing Street (OFF WHITEHALL; CHARING CROSS OR WESTMINISTER UNDERGROUND): You'll have to settle for a distant, partial view of the traditional home of the prime minister for the past two-and-a-half centuries. Still, it's an almost compulsary stop for any visitor to London, so political-science students can hardly pass it by. Don't make cracks about IRA bombs in earshot of the officers guarding the gate.

Mansion House (NEAR THE INTERSECTION OF THREADNEEDLE AND CORNHILL STREETS; BANK UNDERGROUND): The Lord Mayor of London lives in Mansion House, which, if not an oxymoron, is certainly a redundancy. Guided tours of the 18th-century building can be arranged, but walk-in visitors will be turned away.

Guildhall (OFF GRESHAM STREET; MONUMENT OR BANK UNDERGROUND): The Guildhall's importance crosses various spheres — politics, economics, history, and architecture. Its significance for students of politics is its role as the city hall of the City of London.

Temple Bar Memorial (FLEET STREET; TEMPLE OR ALDWYCH UNDERGROUND): There's not much to see, but the significance of Temple Bar Memorial bears reflecting on. This entrance to the City of London is marked by an 1880 stone pedestal topped by a bronze griffin, the symbol of the City. From 1672 to 1878, a gateway designed by architect Christopher Wren marked this boundary between Westminster and the City. To this day, the monarch is not allowed to enter the City unless invited to do so by the Lord Mayor of London.

Suffragette Memorial (VICTORIA TOWER GARDENS; WESTMINSTER UNDERGROUND): The memorial pays tribute to Emmeline Pankhurst and her daughter Christabel Pankhurst, leaders of the Suffragette struggle for women's rights in the early 20th century.

London Dungeon (34 TOOLEY STREET; LONDON BRIDGE UNDERGROUND): The word that leaps to mind in trying to describe the London Dungeon is *American*. There is something very American about the approach taken in this fun but not very authentic-feeling attraction. You leave the Dungeon half expecting to find yourself at Disney World or a Six Flags amusement park. The Dungeon, however, does make you reflect on the terrible conditions and torture that made imprisonment a living hell for many people.

The Clink Exhibition (CLINK STREET; CANNON STREET, MONUMENT OR LONDON BRIDGE UNDERGROUND): Fans of *Hogan's Heroes* might be disappointed at the lack of connection to the TV stalag's colonel (nudge, nudge, wink, wink). The Clink Exhibition, near the site of a particularly grim 16th-century prison, offers a look at the lives of those who ran afoul of the law and paid the price.

The House of Detention (CLERKENWELL CLOSE; FARRINGDON UNDERGROUND): Prisons have stood here for more than three centuries. Underground cells give you an idea of the hardships prisoners endured.

Tyburn Gallows (MARBLE ARCH UNDERGROUND): A grim legacy mars the beauty of Marble Arch. Tyburn Gallows, where executions were carried out from 1196 to 1783, was located on what is today the site of Marble Arch. Look for the stone memorial on the site of "Tyburn Tree," a permanent gallows that stood from 1571 to 1759.

Jack the Ripper Walk: Step back into time and explore the murders that terrified Londoners in 1888. One of the most popular guided walks offered by The Original London Walks tour company (telephone: 0171-624-3978) is *Jack the Ripper's London*. This nighttime exploration of the murder sites and suspects may leave you a bit unnerved, but you're sure to finish the evening with your throat intact.

Museum of London (LONDON WALL; BARBICAN UNDERGROUND): An exhibit in this museum tracing the history of London gives you a glimpse of 18th-century prison cells.

Scotland Yard: The headquarters of the Metropolitan Police Force, New Scotland Yard, built in 1967, is on Victoria Street (ST. JAMES PARK UNDERGROUND). A blue plaque in Whitehall Place marks the site of Old Scotland Yard, the headquarters of the Metropolitan Police from 1829 to 1890 (CHARING CROSS UNDERGROUND).

Metropolitan Police Historical Museum (28 BOW STREET; COVENT GARDEN UNDERGROUND): Exhibits in this museum, located in the Bow Street Police Station, across from the Royal Opera House, trace the history of London's police. You can only visit by appointment, so put your request to the museum in writing.

Chapter 13

Business and Economics

A global center of banking and finance and home to countless multinational companies, London teems with contemporary points of interest for students of business and economics. Of course, London's global influence in business and economics goes back centuries, so there are many historical connections to make as well. After all, this was the heart of one of the greatest empires in the history of the world. And here lived Karl Marx and Margaret Thatcher, not to mention numerous others whose ideas transformed the economy of Britain or the world.

THE LONDON EXPERIENCE
Standing the Test of Time

James Smith & Sons seems an anachronism, occupying the corner of Bloomsbury Street and New Oxford Street in a bustling area of London where the 20th century is writ large (TOTTENHAM COURT ROAD UNDERGROUND). But this umbrella shop is a world apart. Large display windows wrap around the facade and distinctively old-fashioned lettering proclaims the shop's name all the way around. More lettering states "Est. 1830" and "Umbrella Stick and Whip Manufacturers." A visitor whose eyes pan along the passing cityscape from an upstairs perch in a double-decker bus or whose gaze roves the surroundings while walking by on the street can't fail to be intrigued. Unlike the tourist, the traveler is guided by the temptation to explore facets of London that challenge, that provoke, that require one to reflect on how this or that fits into the fabric of the city. The traveler goes beyond the Disney World impressions afforded by the touring mentality that sweeps in the Tower of London, Westminster Abbey, and little else that's not in everyone's list of Top 10 things to do in London.

Why an umbrella shop? Why here? How many kinds of umbrellas can there be? How has it lasted for over a century and a half?

Such questions resound in your mind when you pass by James Smith & Sons umbrella shop. Go in and answer those questions. Better yet, go in, look around, and tell an employee that you are a foreign student of business or economics and you would like to know more about their shop and the business it generates. The staff is almost certain to be pleased and proud that you have such an interest in their shop. They'll probably talk your ear off. And that's the idea.

In James Smith & Sons, you'll find a great selec-

tion of sturdy, occasionally elegant, handmade umbrellas of such quality that they seem only distantly related to the flimsy contraptions that most of us wave in vain at stormy skies, ultimately only provoking the gods of wind and rain to buffet our overmatched shields into something that hints at Picasso's cubist sensibilities — two exposed prongs here, an upturned bit of fabric there, a tear in the middle where drops begin to form and plop down onto your nose. James Smith & Sons sells umbrellas fit for a king — or at least a viscount. The prices may or may not cause you to gasp, but the principle of "you get what you pay for" becomes abundantly clear when the helpful staff demonstrates the shop's wares.

Although umbrellas are the stock in trade, James Smith & Sons also has a wide range of walking sticks for people of all fashion sensibilities. Indeed, one of the authors suffered a painful leg injury in London a few years ago. The staff at James Smith & Sons spent a full hour fitting him with a walking stick perfectly balanced to his hand and of the perfect length.

Tucked into London's nooks and crannies, you'll find other such specialty shops that have stood the test of time. For a student of business or economics, spending a free day or a half-day after classes exploring a handful of these shops is a wonderful way to see a real-world application of various aspects of product development, quality control, distribution and marketing, and customer relations. This exploration will also give you pause for thought about the British love for tradition and the extent of British political and economic influence in the 19th and 20th centuries. These places are a bit like dinosaurs, but they are not in some marketing *Jurassic Park*. These dinosaurs never died out — they survived and they exude the lost world.

The perfect second stop would be **Twining's Tea Shop,** located near where the Strand becomes Fleet Street at the Temple Bar Monument (TEMPLE UNDERGROUND). Look carefully, or you might miss Twining's, the narrowest shop in London. Step into the shop, and you feel as if you've been transported back to the 18th century, when Twining's opened on this site. Variety upon variety of tea lines the walls, and the firm's owners through the ages peer at you with their oil-painting gaze from ornate frames. The staff is subdued, almost as if they don't want to disturb tea lovers' reverie as those buyers make the critical selection. But if you inquire further about their goods or the shop, they'll gladly regale you with observations and facts.

Your third destination should be **Lock & Co.** hat makers in St. James near the intersection of St. James Street and King Street (PICCADILLY CIRCUS UNDERGROUND).

Bowlers, boaters, and other fine gentlemen's hats have been meticulously hand-crafted by Lock & Co. since 1700. After three centuries of fitting heads, Lock & Co. can certainly take care of yours.

Lock & Co. is a good place to leave you because this posh area abounds with small shops where traditional craftsmanship prevails. Poke around and reflect on the endurance of quality and just how far from Wal-Mart you are.

If you decide you want to track down other venerable and uniquely British shops, try the following for starters.

Floris, Ltd. (89 JERMYN STREET; PICCADILLY CIRCUS UNDERGROUND): This elegant shop, opened in 1730, is one of London's finest vendors of perfume, cologne, and all manner of fragrant toiletries for women and men. Floris holds royal warrants, which designate a company as an official purveyor of goods to the Royal Family.

Toye, Kenning & Spencer (GREAT QUEEN STREET; COVENT GARDEN UNDERGROUND): This company, which dates back to 1685, was given the Royal Warrant for Gold and Silver Laces, Insignia, and Embroidery for its embroidery on Queen Elizabeth's coronation gown in 1952. Here you'll find military braid and buttons, uniform badges, trophies, figurines, and all manner of things.

ON DISPLAY
The Bank of England Museum

The Bank of England Museum (BARTHOLOMEW

LANE; BANK UNDERGROUND) reminds you of money, money, money at every turn — and the fact that you wish you had more of it. Your pangs of monetary yearning peak when you stand in front of the gold bullion bars that are displayed altar-like at the core of the museum. You may find yourself looking around the room to gauge the level of security as the movie reel of your mind plays a scene in which you are dressed in form-fitting black, only your eyes showing, sliding down a rope, deftly dodging the spiderweb of laser beams that surround the gold display. Snap out of it!

Exhibits at the Bank of England Museum trace the origins of the British monetary system, the emergence of banks, and the creation of the Bank of England. The story of the Bank of England up to the modern era is methodically told with interesting displays. The museum, which is located within the mammoth Bank of England building, whose imposing facade is on Threadneedle Street, succeeds in piquing the visitor's interest and maintaining it. Nothing would have been easier than designing a deadly dull ho-hummer of a banking museum. Gratefully, the creators of the Bank of England Museum have laid out a user-friendly museum for visitors of all ages.

COOL CORNERS

Burlington Arcade (PICCADILLY; PICCADILLY CIRCUS UNDERGROUND) charms visitors to London with its old-world sensibility. The student of business, however, can study Burlington Arcade as a 19th-century predecessor of today's shopping malls. The decidedly upscale shops specialize in jewelry, fine art, leather goods, fine writing utensils and clothing, among other items.

Burlington Arcade, built in 1819, extends from Piccadilly to Burlington Gardens, running along the west side of Burlington House, where the Royal Academy is located. Look for the security guards, known as Beadles, whose quaint attire, replete with top hat, makes them seem like time travelers.

STREET STUDY
Streets of Gold

The heart of the financial district beckons students of business and economics. Start your street study by taking the Tube to Bank Station. After you emerge from the Underground, you'll find yourself at the convergence of Cornhill and Threadneedle. The building in the triangle formed by the convergence of the two streets formerly housed the Royal Exchange. The massive building across the way on Threadneedle is the Bank of England, whose museum was described above.

First cross over to the peninsula where the old **Royal Exchange** stands. The bronze horseman at the tip of the peninsula is the Duke of Wellington. The present building was actually the third Royal Exchange on this site. The first, built in 1566, was destroyed one hundred years later

by the Great Fire. The second was destroyed by fire in 1838. The present building became the headquarters of the London International Financial Futures Exchange in 1982.

Take advantage of the benches in front of the Royal Exchange to sit for 5 or 10 minutes — the tranquility here belies the hustle and bustle of the financial district. This is a lovely spot to take it all in.

Look across at the **Bank of England** — you can hardly avoid this because the mammoth, formidable structure commands your attention. The present Bank was begun in 1924, largely replacing its predecessor, designed by the famed architect Sir John Soane. Cross Threadneedle and walk along the Bank's facade.

Turn left on Bartholomew Lane and walk down a block to Throgmorton Street, where you'll find the front of the former **London Stock Exchange** (No. 8). This last Stock Exchange building, built in 1972, was only in service for two decades.

If all this walking and neck-craning stirs your appetite or whets your thirst, it's time to seek out the **Jamaica Wine House** in St. Michael's Alley. The Jamaica Wine House is a fine destination, if for no other reason than it's almost unreasonably hard to find, and there's nothing like a good challenge. But there is another reason. The Jamaica Wine House, reputedly the site of London's first coffee house, was a meeting place for traders. At midday, this pub can be extraordinarily busy, with dark-suited/skirted bankers, stock traders, and others from the financial world spilling out of the pub into the alleyway.

IMMERSION

The Festival of Guilds

If you're in London in the summer, plan to attend the Livery Companies' Exhibition, held at the **Guildhall** off of Gresham Street (BANK UNDERGROUND). The 15th-century Guildhall is essentially the city hall of the City of London — here the Court of Common Council meets and here the Lord Mayor is installed.

The festival, held in mid-July, is a lively and colorful exposition of the skills and artistry of guilds, the forerunners of contemporary trade unions. The displays run the gamut from the traditional to high-tech. In the plaza in front of the Guildhall, you can see demonstrations of sheep-shearing, wooden ship-building, copper pot-making, and the like. Inside the packed Great Hall, some guilds use slick promotional materials to inform visitors about their activities while others (the ones that make less of a mess than their counterparts that shoot arrows or work with live animals) demonstrate *their* trades. You might see someone from the Goldsmith's Guild . . . *gilding* something!

A nice follow-up would be to stroll around the area, trying to locate the headquarters of the various guilds and admiring their buildings and signs. Knock on the doors of one or two — you just might be admitted if you express admiration or curiosity. Dozens of guild headquarters are near Guildhall. Among those you may encounter are Goldsmiths' Hall, Haberdashers' Hall, and Brewers' Hall to the west; Girdlers' Hall and Armourers' Hall to the north; Carpenters' Hall, Drapers' Hall, and Merchant Taylors' Hall to the east; and Grocers' Hall and Mercers' Hall to the south.

THE CROWN JEWELS

Harrods (BROMPTON ROAD; SOUTH KENSINGTON UNDERGROUND) and **Fortnum & Mason** (PICCADILLY; PICCADILLY CIRCUS UNDERGROUND): Whether or not you give a jot about shopping, you should visit these monuments to consumerism. Their buildings and decors are so grandiose, their range of products so diverse, their atmospheres so redolent with an air of shopper exhilaration that they must be experienced. Go without the objective of purchase. Go to take in this feast for the eyes and to observe the shoppers and the salespeople. The food halls alone rank among the most interesting places in London. With an array of goods ranging from the finest chocolates to fresh game to choice caviar to premium wines, the food halls will dazzle your senses. The displays of scrumptious delicacies summon forth a primeval tug of unabashed gluttony. In the self-restraint mode, hand firmly held on your wallet or purse, wander from department to department in these magnificent stores.

Harrods traces its origins to a small grocery shop opened in 1849 by the tea merchant Henry Charles Harrod. Consider it the upstart of the two — Fortnum & Mason is *a century and a half older*, having been founded in 1707.

SHERLOCK SUGGESTS . . .

Smithfield Market (WEST SMITHFIELD; BARBICAN UNDERGROUND): Who would expect a huge meat and poultry market in the middle of a metropolis like London? But here it is.

Lloyds of London (LIME STREET; MONUMENT UNDERGROUND): The headquarters of the renowned underwriters is this architectural perplexity, which looks a bit like a missile launch site. Lloyds dates to the 17th century, while the building belongs to a forbidding future. Fans of *Star Trek* might mistake the building for a Borg spaceship.

London School of Economics (HOUGHTON STREET; TEMPLE OR ALDWYCH UNDERGROUND): This world-renowned university was founded in 1895. Today it is part of the University of London.

Residence of J. M. Keynes (46 GORDON SQUARE; EUSTON UNDERGROUND): The influential economist lived at this address. His house was a gathering place for members of the Bloomsbury Group of writers.

London Silver Vaults (53–65 CHANCERY LANE; CHANCERY LANE UNDERGROUND): Antique silver is sold and stored here.

Inland Revenue (THE STRAND; ALDWYCH OR TEMPLE UNDERGROUND): The government tax-collection department is located in Somerset House. Of course visiting the Courtauld Institute Galleries, also located in Somerset House, is loads more fun than ruminating on taxes.

Old Treasury (WHITEHALL; CHARING CROSS UNDERGROUND): Built in 1845, the Old Treasury was just the latest in a series of treasuries on this site going back to the 16th century.

Custom House (LOWER THAMES STREET; MONUMENT UNDERGROUND): In the Custom House, completed in 1817, a small museum has displays dealing with smuggling, fraud, and other illegal activities that fall under the domain of Customs and Excise.

Chapter 14

History and Military Science

If you're coming to London to study history or military science, it almost seems redundant to go to class. No, we'll get into trouble with our own students if we say that. It's true, though, that you seemingly are confronted by historically significant people, places, and events around every London corner.

Libraries of books have been written about the city's historical significance, so we won't rehash the obvious. In this chapter, we'll discuss the place in a way that will help you get behind the lists of dates and events that typically inhabit the pages of history books. We'll keep the focus on the way people lived, which is, after all, the most interesting part of the study of the subject.

THE LONDON EXPERIENCE
Hampton Court Palace

Our first stop isn't really in Central London at

all, but it's so close, and so bound up with the city's history, that it might as well be. **Hampton Court** is an easy half-hour train ride from Waterloo Station or a pleasant two-hour boat trip from Westminster Pier. We recommend taking the boat, the way King Henry VIII would have, for a unique view of the surrounding countryside. The train station is just across a bridge and a few hundred yards from the palace entrance, while the boat docks at the palace's own pier. Either way, arriving at the palace will make you feel like you've slipped more than 400 years back in time.

Hampton Court is best known as the favorite residence of Henry VIII, but its earliest parts were built by Thomas Wolsey, the Archbishop of York, beginning in 1514. Henry made Wolsey his chancellor and the pope made him a cardinal. When Henry remarked that it just didn't seem right that his chancellor had a finer residence than he, the king, had, Wolsey ingratiated himself with the monarch by giving him the house as a gift.

Generosity didn't do Wolsey much good in the long run. Within five years, the cardinal was out of favor for failing to persuade the pope to grant Henry a divorce. Wolsey probably escaped execution only by having the good sense to die before the headsman could get to him.

This unpleasantness didn't sour Henry on the palace, however. He and his second queen, Anne Boleyn, were happy here — for awhile. Like some great schoolboy carving his sweetheart's initials in a tree, Henry had Anne's initials placed at the top of an archway leading into an inner courtyard. Henry proposed to his next wife, Jane Seymour, at Hampton Court, even before Anne met her doom. But he didn't carve initials in the masonry for any more of his half-dozen wives.

Anyway, the palace was a favorite of monarchs for 200 years, being far enough from London to have some quiet and to be mostly out of harm's way whenever the citizens were restless, which was much of the time, yet near enough to get the news and keep Londoners from getting nasty democratic ideas. Each ruler added his or her personal stamp to the place, and extensive building was done by Sir Christopher Wren under William and Mary in the late 1600s.

George III preferred Windsor Castle to Hampton Court, however, so for the past 200 years, the palace has not been a royal residence. Queen Victoria opened it to the public in 1838.

A feeling of history envelops you here. If you sit in the ancient cobblestoned Clock Court in the long shadows of early morning or late afternoon when few other people are about, it's very easy to imagine mail-clad knights on horseback riding past. There are ghosts inside the palace, you'll be told, but this seems an even more likely spot to encounter one.

Begin your tour in the royal kitchens and marvel at how Henry's staff managed to whip up a daily banquet for the 2000 courtiers who were often in residence. Denizens of the palace consumed more than 8000 sheep, 2000 deer, 1800 pigs, 1200 oxen, tons of fish, and 600,000 barrels of beer a year! There's a free audio tour of the kitchens, and while most audio tours are pretty cheesy, this one's really good and makes the place come alive.

There are a lot of other things to see and do inside this palace. You can walk through the opulence of the 17th-century Royal Apartments or visit an important art gallery. By all means, go into the ornate chapel with its beautifully carved dark wood interior. But beware! The ghost of Henry's fifth queen, Catherine Howard, reputedly walks the nearby corridors, calling for her husband. We've never seen her, but it's just the sort of setting a ghost *would* inhabit!

You can spend all day in the palace itself, but that would be a shame because there's so much to see on the grounds. England's most famous maze is across the lawn, and you can get gleefully turned around in minutes. We've been through it several times, and either everybody gets out OK eventually, or the groundskeepers remove the parched bones of unsuccessful explorers each evening after the visitors go home.

Stop in at the indoor tennis court of Henry VIII, the oldest in the world — or second oldest, depending on whether you accept Oxford's competing claim. You'll probably see some of the locals playing "real tennis" — the ancestor of the game we know today, a sort of odd combination of tennis and squash.

Take a relaxing stroll through the gardens, some of the most lovely in England, and visit the Great Vine, which was planted in 1768 and can produce more than a ton of grapes each year. In a country filled with important historical sites, few are more evocative of the past than Hampton Court Palace. Until science perfects a time machine, a visit to this historic home of kings is one of the best ways we know of to slip four centuries or more into the past.

ON DISPLAY
The Tower

The **Tower of London** (TOWER HILL UNDERGROUND) is more than just a tower — it's a whole complex of buildings. It's been a castle, a royal palace, a prison, an active military base, a mint, and a zoo. In a real sense, it has been a self-contained city during much of its history.

The Tower is thoroughly covered in just about every book about London, and there's a reason for it: it's the most fascinating, historic place in the city. William the Conqueror began building it shortly after invading the country in 1066, and kings and queens made it one of their principal residences for the next 500 years. Absolutely *everything* has happened here — the martyrdom of saints, the assassination of kings, the beheading of queens, imprisonment, torture, thrilling escapes. We can't overstate its historical or military significance.

The best way to get a general familiarity with the place is to take a free tour from one of the guards just inside the entrance. The 45-minute tour gives you an entertaining mix of the essential history and legend of the Tower and shows you a few of the interesting places in the complex.

After the tour, explore on your own. The White Tower is the castle keep in the middle. There are wonderful collections of arms and armor here, with some important pieces and some oddities. There's a huge suit of armor worn by Henry VIII, and a tiny one, evidently made for a child or a dwarf. Look for the weapon that's a combination rifle and crossbow. After your powder and arrows were exhausted, we suppose you could bludgeon the enemy with it!

The upper chamber of the Beauchamp Tower is covered with graffiti etched into the stone walls by centuries of prisoners who were kept there waiting for re-

lease — or for the headsman. Hundreds of people were imprisoned here, and many innocent people spent their last days here before being led to the block just outside the window, where they'd watched other victims, guilty and innocent alike, lose their lives.

There's more to do: walk along the ramparts for a stirring view of the river and Tower Bridge, visit the numerous other chambers and dungeons, pause in the quiet and elegant Chapel of St. John to reflect on those who gave their lives here for principle, and, of course, see the opulent display of the Crown Jewels and Coronation Robes. Lines into the Jewel House are quite long on summer afternoons, so visit this exhibit first thing in the morning.

Every place you put your feet, as you stride through the grounds of this fabulous place, is ground trod by the famous and powerful of the last thousand years. Perhaps the ghosts that surround you here will inspire you to become another of the great men and women who have spent time in the Tower!

COOL CORNERS

Probably the two mightiest and most influential realms in Western civilization have been the Roman and British empires. These were not mere military conquests; they shaped the course of history, culture, and even thought for centuries after they were gone. That's probably one of the reasons you've come to London. Here are three ways to spend an afternoon in the living past.

Searching for Roman Ruins: Caesar invaded

Britain and Claudius finally held it for Rome, and although the Romans pulled out more than 1500 years ago, traces of them are everywhere. You can begin at the **Tower** and take a well-marked two-mile walk that will trace the path of the wall the Romans built around Londinium, ending at the Museum of London. You'll see sections of the **Roman Wall** and traces of gates and forts on your stroll, part of which is along a street called, of all things, London Wall.

The remains of the **Temple of Mithras,** the preferred god of Roman soldiers, were discovered by builders in 1954 near Leadenhall and Cornhill streets in the City and have been reconstructed nearby. Also check out the crypt at **St. Bride's** on Fleet Street for a Roman pavement and remains of another temple.

The Cabinet War Rooms (KING CHARLES STREET; WESTMINSTER OR CHARING CROSS UNDERGROUND): On your walk down Whitehall, you'll find a discreet sign pointing you down King Charles Street to this attraction. This is the bunker where Winston Churchill spent much of World War II meeting with his generals and planning strategy and from which he made countless morale-boosting addresses to the British people. After the war the rooms were left as they were at the time and sealed, only to be reopened a generation later. Nearly 20 rooms of this underground complex are open, and they provide a glimpse of how the wheels of government were kept in motion in the face of saturation bombing.

The Royal Hospital and National Army Museum (ROYAL HOSPITAL ROAD; SLOANE SQUARE UNDERGROUND): The Royal Hospital was set up in Chelsea by

Charles II in the 1660s and has been caring for Army pensioners ever since. These men still stride the grounds in their distinctive red jackets and are happy to tell stories (most of them true!) of the area, the army, and themselves. If you have an interest in oral history or military movements as seen by the guys on the front lines, this is the place to come and listen. The grounds are lovely, and the interiors of many of the buildings are striking.

Next door is the National Army Museum, which commemorates the battles and regiments that made the British Empire a globe-spanning force. Don't be put off by the huge, ugly chunk of graffiti-covered concrete in front: That's one of their more recent and significant exhibits — a section of the Berlin Wall.

Street Study
Parliament Square and Whitehall

London, of course, oozes history from every pore. Some parts of the city, though, do more than ooze. The Parliament Square and Whitehall area is such a place. History gushes, spurting unchecked from every doorway! Take this easy half-hour walk and you'll be drenched in it.

Begin behind Westminster Abbey, across the busy street from the Houses of Parliament. We talk more about Parliament in chapters 11 and 12 and more about the Abbey in Chapter 9, but for now we'll concentrate on the historical associations that fall within your gaze.

Down the street to your right, on your side of the

street, is a boxy-looking stone building called the **Jewel Tower.** It was built in 1365 to store the treasures of King Edward III and was later used as a records storehouse by Parliament and as the Office of Weights and Measures. There's a nice display there now on the history of Parliament. (THERE'S MORE ABOUT THE JEWEL TOWER IN CHAPTER 12.)

Behind you, of course, is **Westminster Abbey,** which is worth mentioning here because of its numerous royal burials and memorials to statesmen, soldiers, and scores of other illustrious historical figures.

Across the street is the **Houses of Parliament,** perhaps the most widely recognized building in the world. Even the frenetic traffic on Abingdon Street won't dim the pleasure you'll have in just standing there on the sidewalk admiring this distinctive building. By London standards, it's not very old. A terrible fire destroyed the previous Palace of Westminster in 1834, and this building, its successor, was complete by 1860. The only remaining part of the older building is the great hall at the far left (north) end, Westminster Hall, which is more than 900 years old.

Stay on the west side of the street and cross the street to Parliament Square, a pleasant little green oasis amidst the exhaust fumes. Near the other end of the square, you'll pass a statue of Sir Winston Churchill. Churchill left strict instructions that no statue be erected in his memory: he said he couldn't abide the knowledge of pigeons doing on *his* head what pigeons do. After the great man's death, a statue was raised anyway — but it's *electrified* to keep the dirty birds away!

Cross the street again and you're on **Whitehall,** synonymous with the seat of the British government. (Actually it's not Whitehall yet, it's still Parliament Street. It changes names in the middle of the block in the capricious way London streets often do.) Worth noting before we go further: there are award-winning public toilets in the pedestrian subway beneath Whitehall, designated in several recent years as the cleanest in the capital. Thought you'd like to know.

The first buildings you pass are the sort of solid, soulless structures you'd expect to be inhabited by bureaucrats, and you'd be right. The Foreign and Home offices and the Treasury have space here. But off to your left is King Charles Street, and at its end are the Cabinet War Rooms we told you about earlier in this chapter. Continue your stroll, noticing the Cenotaph, an important war memorial, in the middle of the street.

The next street is **Downing Street;** the home of the prime minister is **No. 10.** A pair of police constables keeps the public from getting any closer, but it's worth loitering here for a bit. You can occasionally see government ministers and dignitaries driving through the great iron gates, and the policemen here always seem to be the most talkative of all London bobbies.

Stroll past the Old Treasury and the Scottish Office and cross at the corner. This is **Banqueting House,** the last remaining building from the old Whitehall Palace of King James I, finished in 1619. A decade later Charles I hired Rubens to paint the ceilings of his palace, and they're still magnificent today. Charles didn't last so long; in 1648, he stepped from a window of this building onto a scaffold to face execution during the English Civil War. (SEE CHAPTER 12 FOR MORE ON BANQUETING HOUSE.)

Back across the street now, to pet the horses on guard outside the **Horse Guards.** Actually, it's the *soldiers* who are on guard, but you mustn't pet them. The Changing of the Guard that takes place in Horse Guards Parade behind this building is less crowded and, in our opinion, more interesting than the more famous change at Buckingham Palace. This one takes place daily at 11 A.M.

Continue up the street for a few more blocks past the Admiralty, from which Britain's naval conquests and empire-building were directed. When you reach the distinctive Admiralty Arch, you're at Trafalgar Square.

IMMERSION
The Keys

We visited the Tower of London a few pages ago, but now we want to go back at night, long after the tourists have gone home. The **Ceremony of the Keys** — the official locking of the Tower — has taken place each night for more than 700 years without a miss for fire, plague, or war. Visitors are admitted by prior arrangement to observe the 20-minute ceremony, which produces a feeling of being an actual part of history. How often do we get to participate in an event that has been going on for seven unbroken centuries?

To obtain a pass, write to:

> The Resident Governor
> H. M. Tower of London
> London EC2
> United Kingdom

List the date you would like to attend and give two or three alternate dates. If you're writing from outside Britain, enclose an International Reply Coupon. Otherwise send a self-addressed, stamped envelope.

Visitors are admitted about 9:30 P.M. and escorted to a viewing area near Traitors' Gate. One of the guards will explain the history and nature of the ceremony, and guests watch it executed — we probably shouldn't use that word here in the Tower! — with the strictest military precision. The Tower is now locked for the night. No one will be allowed in or out except your party of viewers, who will be shown out through a concealed door.

THE CROWN JEWELS

The Museum of London (LONDON WALL; BARBICAN UNDERGROUND): One of the best places to learn about London is at the museum dedicated to the history of the city. London life is displayed through artifacts and exhibits from early Roman times into the 20th century, and special exhibitions highlight the Great Plague of 1665 and the Great Fire of 1666.

The Imperial War Museum (LAMBETH ROAD; LAMBETH NORTH UNDERGROUND): Despite its name, this museum is anything but a glorification of war. On the contrary, it is very touching in its presentations of the effects of war on both soldiers and civilians. On our last visit we saw a burly college man literally moved to tears by its depiction of the carnage of World War I. Visitors can experience the discomfort of World War I trenches, the terror of living in a London bomb shelter during the Blitz, or the horror of concentration camps. There's plenty of military strategy in sight, but it's a museum that will appeal both to war heroes and to pacifists — quite a feat!

The Victoria and Albert Museum (CROMWELL ROAD; SOUTH KENSINGTON UNDERGROUND): London's great lumber-room of an attic, the Victoria and Albert Museum is absolutely filled with this and that! The V&A holds a vast collection that traces fashion through the last four centuries, magnificent cartoons (painted models) for enormous tapestries by Raphael, breathtaking collections of jewelry, armor, and Chinese art. Here are collections of furniture, Islamic art, and models by Frank Lloyd Wright, as well as extensive displays of old musical instruments, stained glass, portrait miniatures, and artifacts too numerous to mention.

SHERLOCK SUGGESTS . . .

Greenwich: For an understanding of the centuries of naval might that created and defended the British Empire over four centuries, take a 12-minute train ride or 45-minute boat trip to Greenwich and visit the **Royal Naval College** and the **National Maritime Museum**. There is much else to see of a non-military nature in Greenwich as well. (THERE'S MORE ABOUT GREENWICH IN CHAPTERS 8 AND 15.)

The HMS *Belfast* (FERRY FROM MORGAN'S LANE; LONDON BRIDGE UNDERGROUND): This World War II cruiser provides a close-up look at modern naval history, from the defense of Britain against the Axis to the war with Argentina over the Falkland Islands. The ship, which is moored on the south side of the Thames just upriver from Tower Bridge, is open daily.

St. Paul's Cathedral (LUDGATE HILL; ST. PAUL'S UNDERGROUND): St. Paul's is famous for its connection with Britain's military heroes. See the monuments and burial vaults of the two greatest of those heroes, Lord Nelson and the Duke of Wellington. The monuments are in the nave and the gravesites are in the crypt. Numerous other stellar military figures are commemorated at St. Paul's. (THERE'S MORE ABOUT ST. PAUL'S EVERYWHERE, BUT ESPECIALLY IN CHAPTERS 8 AND 9.)

Temple Church (MIDDLE TEMPLE; TEMPLE UNDERGROUND): This historic building, located just south of Fleet Street a hundred yards through Temple Gateway, is an ancient round church, built in 1160, which contains the effigies of crusaders of the period. Off the usual tourist tracks, the church is seldom visited but offers a quiet and historical respite from the bustle of the nearby City. (THERE'S MORE ABOUT TEMPLE CHURCH IN CHAPTER 12.)

Highgate Cemetery (HIGHGATE UNDERGROUND): The last resting place of many of London's most famous figures is a short Tube ride north of the city. Great figures in every line of endeavor are buried here: politics (Karl Marx), literature (George Eliot), science (Michael Faraday), and countless others.

Chapter 15

The Physical Sciences

Students of literature, theatre, law, and business think of London as their exclusive intellectual preserve. They're wrong. They walk the streets muttering Shakespearean sonnets, spend hours at the ticket booth in Leicester Square, watch judges in odd costumes at work in Old Bailey courtrooms, or gaze in orgasmic delight at the great bronze doors of the Bank of England. And all the while they never realize they're in the city of Isaac Newton, Michael Faraday, and Edmund Halley.

And if they knew, they'd probably have no clue who those guys were, anyway.

You, on the other hand, know that television began here, not in America; that Thomas Edison's light-bulb was . . . uh, "invented" almost 20 years after it was done here; and that all the world's time and geographic location are based on standards set here.

London, for reasons we've never understood,

doesn't trumpet its scientific connections the way it features its literary and historical associations, but there's plenty to see and do here. Come with us on a tour of Scientific London.

THE LONDON EXPERIENCE
The Old Royal Observatory

Take a step to where Time began. No, we're not talking about archeology: we mean the *measurement* of time. The English didn't invent timekeeping, of course, nor the 24-hour clock. But the idea for a fixed standard time is rooted in Greenwich, on the southeast side of Greater London. All timekeeping is based on *Greenwich Mean Time*, now often called Universal Coordinated Time.

The English weren't concerned so much with making sure the trains ran on time; it was another form of transportation entirely that lead them to standardize timekeeping and geographic measurement — sailing ships. The British were developing the world's richest and most far-flung empire, and accurate measurement of both the time and the Earth were crucial to getting their ships where they wanted them to go, especially getting them there ahead of those of the Spanish, the Portuguese, and everybody else. So, precise navigation became necessary to enlarge and protect the empire.

North-south navigation was no problem because bearings to determine latitude could be taken from the sun in the daytime and the North Star at night. But determining east-west location was much more difficult because there are no fixed celestial reference points that could permit this.

King Charles II created the **Royal Observatory** in Greenwich to tackle the problem in 1674, just the point in time at which the increasing volume of trade with the New World and the Orient made a solution critical. John Flamsteed was appointed the first astronomer royal, and the king's friend Christopher Wren was engaged to build an observatory. The result was what is now called Flamsteed House.

Take the boat from Westminster Pier near the Houses of Parliament on a trip down to Greenwich. This route is easy enough to navigate — the captain just floats downriver until he gets there — but it seems a fitting homage to the astronomers who worked out the system of longitude and precision clocks that made oceanic navigation possible.

A straight line can be measured by starting at one end and stopping at the other. But to measure a sphere — Earth, for example — you must choose an arbitrary starting point. Flamsteed chose Greenwich. That starting point for measuring — zero degrees longitude — was

used by the British Navy as the baseline for identifying all longitudinal coordinates. Flamsteed's line was modified slightly by subsequent astronomers royal, and in 1884 the line of Sir George Airy was recognized as the Prime Meridian of the world.

Standard Time came from Greenwich, too, because of the need of mariners to find their precise position at sea. With 18th-century sextants, mariners could tell how far fixed celestial objects were above the horizon. Navigational tables told how high those objects were above the horizon at specific times at Greenwich. So if they knew what time it was at Greenwich, they could easily calculate their distance from the Greenwich Meridian — their longitude. They therefore needed timepieces that accurately kept the time of a particular place — Greenwich. Greenwich standard time became more important to sailors than the local time wherever they were.

The struggle to create a timepiece that could keep accurate time over the weeks and months of a rolling, pitching, tossing, bounding (erp!) sea voyage took decades of work and was beset by intrigue and politics. Many exhibits in the Observatory recount this effort and show the workings of the once super-secret models of watches that tried and failed to make the grade.

Since so many of the ensuing navigational charts were used worldwide, Greenwich time became an important international standard, and other places gradually fixed their own local times according to their relation to Greenwich. Within a few years the speed of rail travel made the establishment of fixed time zones a necessity. Railway timetables, for example, would have been impossible to create with every town operating on a slightly different time based on the local observation of noon. It became reasonable to make Greenwich, which stood at zero degrees longitude, the place from which time zones were measured. Time, as we measure it, literally begins at Greenwich.

Incidently, while you're in Greenwich, do feel free to have your photo taken strad-dling the Prime Meridian, one foot in each hemisphere. Maybe you'll be the billionth tourist to do so — they're surely getting close to that number by now — and win a round-the-world cruise or something equally appropriate. (THERE'S MORE ABOUT GREENWICH IN CHAPTER 8.)

ON DISPLAY
The Science Museum

If there's a more exciting place than the **Science Museum** (EXHIBITION ROAD; SOUTH KENSINGTON UNDERGROUND) to learn about science and technology, we haven't found it — not in London, not anywhere. No matter what branch of science you're studying, this is a museum you mustn't miss.

Your first item of business after entering the museum should be to turn right and walk up the stairs to the mezzanine, where you'll find the Synopsis Gallery — sort of the *Reader's Digest* Condensed Version of the museum. This gallery gives you a quick overview of what's here and where to find it. While many of the exhibits in the museum are hands-on demonstrations geared toward younger students, even the most sophisticated doctoral candidates will find hours of fascinating exhibitions here.

We think that the chemistry section on the second floor, which focuses on work in the laboratory and features the work of seven Nobel Prize winners, is especially strong. The chemical technology and petrochemistry sections are extensive. Nearby is a comprehensive history of weights and measures, including the measure that for many years was used as the world standard metre, and a comprehensive gallery devoted to nuclear physics.

On the third floor are marvelous galleries on optics, temperature, geophysics, and oceanography, each among the world's most complete.

We can't even begin to give you the flavor of this museum. Its collections are too extensive. We take our own students here for the communication technology — both printing and broadcasting — and the engineering students have much to see as well. Computer-science students can see Babbage's Engine, the world's first calculating machine. This is the ideal place for you to spend your first rainy afternoon in London, and you'll probably want to return throughout your stay.

COOL CORNERS

National Portrait Gallery (ST. MARTIN'S PLACE; CHARING CROSS OR LEICESTER SQUARE UNDERGROUND): All the greats of England are depicted here, of course, but this is the place to pay particular homage to all the notable scientists and engineers who invented the modern world. The museum is arranged chronologically, so you start on the top floor and work your way down to the present time. In addition, rooms are thematic. When you reach Room 14 on Level 4, for example, you're in the Science and Industrial Revolution Room, where you can see contemporary portraits of steam-engine inventor James Watt, tunnel builder I. K. Brunel, railway developer George Stephenson, and numerous other scientists and inventors.

Room 16 on Level 3 is set aside for Victorian Science and Technology. Here you can meet Darwin, Huxley, Faraday, and the forgotten Joseph Swan, whose invention of the electric light predated Edison's by two decades. No one actually claims that Edison stole Swan's work, because he was conducting his own independent line of research. But Edison *did* see an article about Swan's early work with carbon filaments — and a British court did find that Edison *had* violated Swan's British patent, which was taken out months before Edison's American one. The court ordered the rival inventors into a partnership in the United Kingdom, at least. (THERE'S MORE ABOUT THE NATIONAL PORTRAIT GALLERY IN CHAPTER 12.)

Bakelite Museum (12 MUNDANIA COURT, FOREST HILL ROAD; HONOR OAK PARK UNDERGROUND): If you looked at the extensive exhibition on plastics at the Science Museum, your next stop should be the Bakelite Museum in East Dulwich. Here are thousands of objects made from plastics of all sorts, especially very early compounds that date from the mid-1800s. The museum also houses a large collection of research materials.

Burlington House (PICCADILLY; PICCADILLY CIRCUS UNDERGROUND): The bustle of Piccadilly fades away as soon as you walk through the arch. This grand building is best known as the home of the Royal Academy of Arts, but it's an important building to the scientific community, too, as the headquarters of a number of learned societies.

The Linnean Society has its quarters here, and its library, which focuses on natural history, evolution, and anthropology, is open to the public. It was here, in fact, that Darwin read his paper that outlined his theory of evolution.

Also housed here are the Geographical Society, the Royal Society (for chemists), and the Royal Astronomical Society. While their quarters are not normally open to the public, your professors may sometimes be able to obtain invitations to lectures for serious students.

STREET STUDY
The Science Capital of Europe

There are two walks on this planet on which you can, within just a few hundred yards, sample humankind's greatest intellectual achievements. One is The Mall, in Washington, DC, home to the Smithsonian Institution. The other is in London, from Cromwell Road, along Exhibition Road, to Kensington Gardens.

This area became the Scientific Capital of Europe because of the Great Exhibition of 1851, the first of the great World's Fairs. Inspired by Prince Albert, the consort of Queen Victoria, the exhibition displayed the best of what the globe-spanning British Empire had to offer. The chief exhibit hall was an enormous glass building, the famous Crystal Palace. After the fair the palace was moved to a south London suburb where it remained until it was destroyed by fire some 80 years later. But the profits from the exhibition stayed at the site: they were used to sponsor the museums that grew up in the area.

The chief museums of the area are described more fully in this and other chapters, but you shouldn't miss the opportunity to start from the South Kensington Tube Station and take in this intellectual theme park. You can get to many of the museums without going above ground. The Tube station opens into a tunnel that takes you under Cromwell Road and leads you to an exit for each of the museums. Unless you're visiting in a sleet storm, though, approach them from above ground so you can see the beautiful architecture, especially that of the Natural History Museum, notable even in this city of beautiful buildings.

As you cross Cromwell Road, the **Natural History Museum** will be on your left and the **Victoria and Albert Museum** on your right. If you're not ducking into one of these museums, walk north along Exhibition Road. You'll pass what was once the entrance to the **Geological Museum,** now merged into the Natural History Museum as its Earth Galleries. Next in line is the **Science Museum.**

Just past the Post Office is Imperial College Road. For a bird's-eye look at the area, turn left here and walk to the 280-foot-tall Queen's Tower, part of the complex of the **Imperial College of Science and Technology.** You're welcome to wander among the buildings and grounds at one of the world's leading scientific universities. The departments here work closely with nearby museums, even sharing library facilities.

Turn left at Kensington Road, and you're just a few steps from the **Royal Geographical Society,** with its statue of explorer David Livingstone out front. The map room is open to the public and is a perfect place to sit down and plan your next London voyage of discovery.

IMMERSION

The Blue Bloods of Science

The **Royal Institution** (21 ALBEMARLE STREET; GREEN PARK UNDERGROUND) is an august body of scientists established by royal charter in 1799, making it the oldest independent research organization in the world. Scientists affiliated with universities normally spend as much time in the classroom as they do in the laboratory, but here at the "RI" the emphasis is on the highest caliber research unfettered by formal teaching obligations.

Most of what the RI does is conducted out of public view, and the Institution itself can seem stuffy and unapproachable to the casual visitor. Most of its facilities are closed to the public, and inquiries from non-scientists are often answered tersely. But this has more to do with understaffing in the public-relations office than it does with highbrow snootiness. The Royal Institution actually has a remarkable record of reaching out, through lectures and conferences, to the general public to enhance its knowledge and appreciation of science.

Its most famous lecture series, however, is the one you're not invited to. The Institution's Friday evening discourses are, well, an institution in themselves. For 150 years the world's finest minds have lectured the members about their specialties, on topics ranging from the human singing voice to rust, providing this elite body with both a breadth and depth of scientific knowledge that is unavailable anywhere else in the world. The evenings look like something out of a period movie. They are quite formal; members attend in evening clothes and sip fine sherry after the lecture. *We* are not invited.

But there are many equally fine events you *can* take part in. Occasional lunchtime lectures are held at the RI's elegantly appointed headquarters at 21 Albemarle Street, just north of Piccadilly. At these events you can mix more informally with leading scientists from a variety of fields and hear discussions of science questions — such as implications of the hole in the ozone layer — that affect everyone, blue-blooded and red-blooded alike.

Tuesday evening discussions at the RI are open to the public as well as to members, are conducted by equally eminent scholars, and cover a wide range of topics. There is no need to book ahead for these. Tea is served at 5:30 and the presentation begins at 6 P.M. There is no charge.

Furthermore, the Institution sponsors conferences on specific themes that are also open to the public. One such two-day conference examined the controversies of modern science. There were sessions on genetics, space exploration, artificial intelligence, and the preservation of endangered species conducted by scientists and authors from around the world. Costs for such special conferences are generally quite low.

If you're in London to study science, you have, through the Royal Institution's public lectures, access to some of the world's finest scientific minds, possibly a few even greater than your professor's back home. The pain of missing one night at the pub will be more than compensated for once you're home and you can casually drop into a conversation: *Yes, when I studied with the great medical pioneer Dr. Seth O'Scope at the Royal Institution* . . . . The looks of respect, or disbelief, on the faces of your friends and professors will be worth what you paid for the trip.

Information about upcoming public events at the Royal Institution can be obtained by calling the organization at 0171-409-2992 or checking its Web page at *http://www.ri.ac.uk* before you come.

THE CROWN JEWELS

The Faraday Museum (21 ALBEMARLE STREET; GREEN PARK UNDERGROUND): In the basement of the Royal Institution is the laboratory of the Institution's most eminent member, Michael Faraday. Faraday's experiments in electromagnetism changed the world, making cheap, plentiful electricity possible through his invention of the electrical transformer, the dynamo, and other revolutionary innovations.

The laboratory, open to the public only on week-day afternoons for a small fee, contains many of Faraday's personal possessions, scientific instruments, and experiments. His contributions to science are carefully explained.

Madam Tussaud's Waxworks and the **Planetarium** (MARYLEBONE ROAD; BAKER STREET UNDERGROUND): The sky shows at the planetarium are spectacular, but the wait for a ticket may be more than you'll feel it's worth. The planetarium is part of the complex that also includes Madam Tussaud's Waxworks, and the lines to get in can stretch for a block. Many people feel Madam Tussaud's is the best thing in London — but at least as many say it's overpriced and overdone. But you can see (almost) face to face a selection of the great scientists of the past, right alongside some of the world's greatest politicians and criminals — and sometimes it's hard to tell which is which. We'd go to the planetarium and skip the waxworks. But we could be wrong.

SHERLOCK SUGGESTS . . .

The Jewel Tower (ABINGDON STREET; WESTMINSTER UNDERGROUND): Follow the street that runs between the Houses of Parliament and the rear of Westminster Abbey for a few hundred yards, and you'll come to this small medieval building that contains, among other things, a selection of the official weights and measures used by early English monarchs. (THERE'S MORE ABOUT THE JEWEL TOWER IN CHAPTERS 12 AND 14.)

Westminster Abbey (WESTMINSTER UNDERGROUND): The Abbey contains an area informally called Scientists' Corner. Sir Isaac Newton is buried here, as is Lord Kelvin, Joule, and more than two dozen other important scientists. (THERE'S MORE ABOUT THE ABBEY THROUGHOUT THE BOOK, BUT ESPECIALLY IN CHAPTER 9.)

Francis Bacon Monument (GRAY'S INN; CHANCERY LANE UNDERGROUND): We once had a science teacher who called Bacon the Father of Science because he embraced the experimental method. There is a memorial to Bacon in one of the Inns of Court, in Holborn. What is Bacon doing here? He was also a lawyer.

Chapter 16

Life Sciences and Medicine

Some student artists are privileged to study in Paris or Florence. Some theology students get to study in Rome. Lucky journalism students may find themselves in Washington, DC. And if you're in any of the biological, medical, or life sciences, perhaps you'll be able to stay awhile in London.

There are other world centers of the biomedical sciences, to be sure, but while some may be stronger in one area or another than London, it's unlikely that anywhere in the world can offer students the array of opportunities for enrichment that London does. That's the great thing about this city: it's world class in just about every area of endeavor you can think of, except maybe baseball. The baseball we've seen played in Hyde Park has been dreadful, but you can have an intellectual ball using London as your base in just about everything else.

Moreover, no one loves the cultivation of the

earth more than the English do. So if your branch of science is botany, you've planted yourself in the right place.

London is the city of Charles Darwin. Penicillin, the most wondrous of modern wonder drugs, came from Alexander Fleming's London labs. Modern nursing was developed here by Londoner Florence Nightingale. Lister's conquest of germs began here.

Yet with all that mind-boggling biomedical talent, the most useful place to the student of life sciences . . . or even the person with only a casual interest . . . or even a person with no interest at all but who has a biology paper to write . . . is a place almost no visitor knows about.

THE LONDON EXPERIENCE

A Warm London Wellcome

No one who's serious about the life sciences should miss a visit to the Wellcome Trust. Henry Wellcome (1853–1936) left his native Wisconsin and adopted England as his home, made a fortune in phamaceuticals, and, wanting to use his money to promote an understanding of health issues and to undertake research in medicine, founded the Wellcome Trust, a foundation

"to benefit mankind." Since it was founded, the Trust has become the world's largest independent medical research philanthropy.

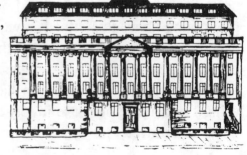

Providing money for medical research — about £250 million per year! — is only a little of what the Trust does. It probably won't give *you* any money. But the other things the Trust does may very well make your life better, and it can certainly enhance your study while you're here.

First of all, there are the exhibits. A permanent exhibition, Science for Life, is housed in the Trust's headquarters at 183 Euston Road (EUSTON OR EUSTON SQUARE UNDERGROUND). Here you can take a close look at how the human body works, with numerous hands-on demonstrations, and walk through a cell enlarged one million times. The gallery has numerous lectures and workshops at all student levels. We observed a workshop on DNA-typing on our last visit.

There are frequent specialized short-term exhibitions as well. "Hospitals in History" examined the role of hospitals as a place of spiritual as well as physical healing. "You Won't Feel a Thing" used a theme of needles to look at topics like vaccination, blood donation, anesthesia, drug abuse, surgery, and acupuncture. Furthermore, across the street at 210 Euston Road, the Trust's 210 Gallery presents moving exhibitions of medical-related art, from computer imagery to paintings on themes ranging from healing to death. All exhibitions are free.

There's more. The **Science Museum** (EXHIBITION ROAD; SOUTH KENSINGTON UNDERGROUND) includes the Museum of Medical History on its fourth and fifth floors. These fascinating exhibits are actually part of the Trust, because Henry Wellcome was intensely interested in the history of the healing arts and was one of the world's great collectors.

These exhibitions can be enjoyed by all students — high school students, college students in any major, graduate students, or medical students — because they contain information at many levels of sophistication. But if you're seriously studying the life sciences in London, you *must* visit their library. Everything you need for your final course paper will be at your disposal here.

The slogan of the library, which is housed in the 183 Euston Road building, is "You need information — We can find it for you." And the staff here is surely the friendliest and most patient in London and seems eager to help with any question, whether the asker walks in, telephones, faxes, or e-mails.

The library's collection is arranged in five sections. The first, Human Biology, is a popular-science collection geared to the general public and a lay audience, not advanced science or medical students or professionals. This section has resources, too, for science teachers at the primary and high school levels.

The second section, Careers and Courses, provides extensive information on science-related careers and education, particularly at British universities. If your summer program has inspired you to apply to a British school next year, this section has all the information you'll need to find a suitable program.

Section three is the much more academic Public Understanding of Science collection. Particularly useful for students, this section deals with attitudes toward science; science in the media, in the arts, and in society;

the nature of science; science and religion; museums; and much more.

Fourth is a large section dealing with Research Ethics. Much more than just a collection of traditional medical-ethics material, this section deals with the social, ethical, and legal implications of all types of scientific research from genetics to animal experimentation.

Finally there is the section on Science Policy. Students seldom use this material because its focus is more on national health plans, health funding and management, and government health legislation. While you may not see many students in this section, you're very likely to see members of Parliament — or at least their research assistants.

Each section includes not only books but also appropriate visual aids from posters to videos, journals, and computer databases, with computers to search both the Internet and databases on CD-ROMs.

If you're studying any science-related material at all in London, but especially if you are studying life sciences, let your research begin here. Chances are it will be the only stop you need to make in writing your papers.

ON DISPLAY
Natural History Museum

London's **Natural History Museum** (CROMWELL ROAD; SOUTH KENSINGTON UNDERGROUND) calls itself "the finest museum of nature in the world." There may be a handful of other museums with the credentials to argue the point, but not many, and they might well lose. The botanist and biologist, the paleontologist and ecologist, the geologist and meteorologist will all find more to see and do here than their trips, however long, can accommodate.

This is a museum that does more than exhibit dinosaurs; it's a working scientific enterprise, one of the most respected in the world. Its exhibits on human biology on the ground floor and evolution on the first floor are especially notable in this city where Darwin himself is buried. And exhibits here demonstrate scientific thinking on evolution that even *anticipated* Darwin by more than 200 years!

The collections of fossils and minerals are vast and breathtaking, and the museum has extensive collections devoted to plant life and marine life.

The Natural History Museum is also headquarters of the International Commission on Zoological Nomenclature, the organization that approves and catalogs the scientific names of all plant and animal life on the planet — fossils as well as current species. Some 15,000 entries are added to the catalog of life on Earth each year. The Commission makes no provision for casual visitors, but visits by serious students can be arranged.

In 1989, the Natural History Museum was consolidated with the Geological Museum next door. The new Earth Galleries are dramatic. One of the most powerful exhibits unlocks the forces within the Earth — volcanoes and earthquakes — and allows you to experience the feeling of being in a quake.

If you're not too shook up after that episode, pay close attention to the 1870s-era building itself. It's a masterpiece. If you think it looks more like a cathedral than it does a museum, you've got a good eye. That was the architect's idea.

COOL CORNERS

Old Operating Theatre Museum (9A ST. THOMAS STREET; LONDON BRIDGE UNDERGROUND): No point in denying it: we've been taking students to London for years, and we know that when they get there, some of them are bound to cut up a little. Here's just the place to do it, although if you are a person of vivid imagination and great sensitivity, it might be better if you stayed away.

This operating room, used from 1821 to 1862, is in the church tower and attic of St. Thomas's Church, the chapel for the ancient St. Thomas's Hospital once

located in the
neighborhood,
and is reached
after a climb
up 32 twisting,
narrow steps.
The room was
used for surgeries
on women, who
were often led into the

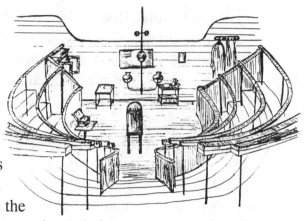

room blindfolded to reduce their terror at seeing the gallery of observers and the horrible instruments. Anesthesia was not used until 1846. A wooden table is at the bottom of a tiered semicircular room arranged so medical students can watch the grisly proceedings. The room has a false floor packed with three inches of sawdust above the true floor — intended to absorb the blood before it can drip down onto the churchgoers below!

You'll also see exhibits of old surgical instruments and techniques. The fainthearted will surely faint.

St. Bartholomew's Hospital (GILTSPUR STREET; BARBICAN OR ST. PAUL'S UNDERGROUND): If it seems so far like most of our recommended stops concern places associated with health care, you're as perceptive as we thought you were when you bought this book. Understanding how our bodies work, and why they sometimes don't, is the essence of the life sciences. So we might as well go all the way and send you to a hospital — a very special hospital.

Bart's, as Londoners call it, is the city's oldest hospital and one of the oldest and most important in the world. It was founded in 1123 by Rahere, a monk who fell ill on a pilgrimage to Rome and regained his health after promising to set up a hospital for the poor. The story of the hospital is told in a small museum just inside the main gate, and it's worth a half-hour of your time to learn how medical practice has advanced in the last 900 years.

Besides the usual terrifying old surgical instruments, you can see hospital records dating back to the 12th century; read a charter signed by Henry VIII; study two world-famous paintings by Hogarth; learn how William Harvey, a physician at Bart's, discovered the circulation of blood; and see many displays demonstrating old health-care practices, like the "lunatic restraints" — leather mittens chained to a heavy belt. Because Bart's is off the usual tourist beat, you may very well have the place to yourself.

Alexander Fleming's Laboratory (ST. MARY'S HOSPITAL, PRAED STREET; PADDINGTON UNDERGROUND): Many of us wouldn't be alive today if it weren't for penicillin, the cornerstone of modern antibiotics. The story of how Fleming discovered penicillin is well known. He had left some experiments sitting in his lab during vacation and when he returned, it looked like, well, perhaps like a college student's kitchen after Spring Break — lots of green things growing where they're not supposed to. As he cleaned up, he noticed that the mold in one neglected petri dish appeared to have inhibited the growth of the bacteria he had been working with. That was all the clue he needed, but it took 13 years before the drug was ready for human use.

Fleming's lab is at St. Mary's Hospital near Paddington Station in a room so small that only a handful of visitors can be accommodated at one time. This lab conveys a good idea of how researchers in many fields work in almost anonymous corners, under spartan conditions, and unlock the amazing secrets that change our lives forever. Fleming's lab is open only from 10 A.M. to 1 P.M., Monday through Thursday.

STREET STUDY
The Best Place in Town To Get Sick

Street names are evocative to Londoners, and are often used as shorthand for an entire idea. Whitehall, as in *News out of Whitehall today focuses on the new poll tax scheme,* implies the national government, even if the news originated in a ministry in an altogether different street. Oxford Street means shopping; Pall Mall refers to the closed, clubby world of men with old money and old vintage port. In the same way, Harley Street is shorthand for practitioners at the top of the medical profession. If you can go to a Harley Street doctor, even if he's located on Wimpole Street, you're getting the best medical care money — a *lot* of money — can buy, because some of the finest doctors in the world practice here.

The Harley Street area, situated just south of Regent's Park, is a medical ghetto. Almost every building is some sort of house of healing with specialists and general practitioners fitted chockablock together. A stroll through the neighborhood will leave you wondering just where all the patients come from. This must be the only place on Earth where doctors' offices outnumber pubs.

Take the Tube to Regent's Park Station, which sits in the middle of Park Crescent. When you alight, walk around to the south side of the crescent and note the **statue of Lord Lister.** Lister, of course, was the first to actually do something about germs. He sterilized surgical instruments, made physicians wash their hands, and invented the idea of antiseptic treatment. While he did most of his work in Edinburgh, this was his London neighborhood.

Walk a block west and you're on **Harley Street.** There are no real tourist attractions along the street, but you'll see building after building where doctors and dentists are at work. If you're passing by the windows here in the winter, when it's dark by 4 o'clock, you can watch people having their blood pressure taken or their teeth being drilled.

As you walk south, **Red Cross House** is at No. 101 Harley Street, and at No. 90 is the site of **Florence Nightingale's original hospital** before she left for the Crimean War, during which she revolutionized nursing. Watch false teeth being made in a basement lab at No. 74.

Where Harley Street dead-ends onto Henrietta Street you'll see the **Royal College of Nursing** on the right. Turn right at this corner and go west one block to Wimpole Street and head back north. Wimpole is one of those odd streets where buildings are numbered consecutively up one side of the street and back down the other, so if you're on the left-hand side of the street the numbers are low and go up. On the right-hand side the

numbers are high and go down. The street brings a ro-
mantic tear to the eye of literature students because of
its association with Elizabeth Barrett and Robert
Browning, but there are more pill-pushers than poets on
the street today.

Lister House is at No. 11–12, and dentists seem
especially thick on the ground in the next few blocks.
The British Dental Association is at No. 64, where
you'll also find a museum illustrating every facet of
dentistry from the 18th century to the present. When
you reach New Cavindish Street, look left to see the
National Heart Hospital a block away, and the King
Edward VII Hospital is a block north of that. The street
ends at Marylebone Road, where you can turn right to
return to Regent's Park Station or left for Baker Street
Station. You've had an invigorating half-hour walk and
feel fine — and if you don't, you couldn't find a better
place in the world to feel ill.

IMMERSION
The Roof Gardens

Let's leave human biology aside for awhile and
turn to botany — or more particularly, gardening. If you
like English gardens, dear reader, the best part of your
life is still ahead of you, because we're going to take
you someplace very special and utterly unique — London's most unexpected garden, perched on a rooftop 100
feet above a busy shopping street.

The Roof Gardens (99 KENSINGTON HIGH STREET;
HIGH STREET KENSINGTON UNDERGROUND) is not a place you
could ever stumble across; it's not easy to find even

when you know what you're looking for. But it's worth the trouble because it is one of London's least-known and most bewitching places. This 1½-acre garden has been on top of a nondescript building for more than 60 years and is a haven of quiet and beauty in the middle of the city. To find it, follow the directions carefully.

Take the Tube to High Street Kensington on the Circle Line. When you emerge from underground, the station opens into a shopping arcade. Walk straight ahead, past the shops, and you'll find yourself on Kensington High Street. Turn right and go east for one block, past the BHS store, to Derry Street. Don't cross any streets, just turn right on Derry and walk down one block to No. 99. There's no sign outside, but if you enter the lobby of this completely uninteresting building, there will be a discreet sign behind the reception desk that says: *Roof Gardens — 6.* You've found it!

The guard at the desk will ask you to sign in and

direct you to the proper lift — the last one on the right. When the door opens into the little lobby, go through the door to the left and emerge into another world!

The Roof Gardens is a fairyland filled with fountains, well-manicured lawns, decorative grasses, flowers that bloom even in December, bridges over quiet ponds stocked with large goldfish, mature trees, and pink flamingoes! It is utterly enchanting! No garden you visit will give you more pleasure than this one. An hour here is the perfect tonic for a body and soul wearied by the noise and bustle of urban life. Visit the Spanish Garden, the Tudor Garden, or the Woodland — an Old English Garden.

You're bound to wonder about the weight of all this. It's considerable, and the roof has been reinforced. The soil is at least 18 inches deep, with rocks below to facilitate drainage. There's a heavy waterproof covering below that to prevent water from seeping through. The water comes from the building's own artesian wells, sunk 500 feet below the building. Each year two tons of mulch and five tons of peat are added to the soil, and the effect is spectacular. The garden requires the services of a head gardener and three full-time assistants.

There's no charge to visit the garden, but there is a members-only restaurant and nightclub up here that operates on Thursday and Saturday nights. The building and garden — which are owned by Sir Richard Branson, who also owns Virgin Airlines, Virgin Records, and most of everything else that's not owned by the Royal Family — is open to the public every day from 9 A.M. to 5 P.M.

THE CROWN JEWELS

London Zoo (REGENT'S PARK): The Zoo almost closed a few years ago, but an 11th-hour infusion of new money saved it. The Zoo is smaller than many famous zoos, but its compactness makes it easy to see on a quiet morning. Its origin dates to the menagerie at the Tower of London, but it has been at its present location since 1828. The Zoo was the site of the first public aquarium (1849), the first reptile house (1853), the first insect house (1881), and the first children's zoo (1938). The most popular attractions now are probably its pandas and the giraffes. The first giraffes were unloaded at the docks along the Thames in 1836 and walked five miles to Regent's Park. Along the way they nearly stampeded in fright at their first sight of a cow in the East End! The Zoo isn't easy to reach by Tube. The nearest stations — Baker Street, Regent's Park, and St. John's Wood — are about a 20-minute walk from the Zoo. But the No. 274 bus from Baker Street makes the trip in minutes.

Kew Gardens (KEW GARDENS UNDERGROUND): This is the largest botanic garden in the world, and an afternoon here is the perfect escape from daily urban turmoil. More than 10 percent of all the world's flowering plant species are represented at Kew, an astonishing record due largely to the efforts of an early director, Sir Joseph Banks. Beginning in 1772, Banks sent collectors to all corners of the far-flung British Empire and beyond, and charged them with bringing back as many examples as possible of Earth's varied plant life.

Kew pays particular attention to endangered

plants, having in some cases the world's only remaining examples of some species, which it tries to propagate and reintroduce into the wild. Scientists there also have an extensive program of screening plants for their medicinal value.

Buildings with carefully controlled environments allow tropical or Alpine plants to thrive in native conditions, so you can see bananas or coffee growing even in the midst of a London winter. If you're in London to study biology or botany, Kew will be one of your most educational visits. For the rest of us, it's just a beautiful and serene day out of central London.

Chelsea Physic Garden (66 ROYAL HOSPITAL ROAD; SLOAN SQUARE UNDERGROUND): A "physic garden" is a place where medicinal plants and herbs were cultivated in earlier times. Many large gardens have sections devoted to herbal medicine, but Chelsea Physic Garden is the most comprehensive one you're likely to find. Set up in 1673 by the Society of Apothecaries, which still owns it, to study the medical properties of plants, it is open only on Wednesday and Sunday afternoons. An extensive research program continues at the garden, and not only its medicinal plants have made a difference in the modern world: the seeds that started the cotton industry in the American South came from this garden. The garden is on Chelsea Embankment, a 15-minute walk from Sloan Square Underground Station. A No. 239 bus from Victoria goes right past it along Royal Hospital Road.

Freud Museum (20 MARESFIELD GARDENS; HAMPSTEAD UNDERGROUND): Sigmund Freud spent most of his life in Vienna, but he lived in London for the final year of his life. This museum in a cheerful village just north of London reviews the life and work of the father of psychoanalysis.

SHERLOCK SUGGESTS . . .

Florence Nightingale Museum (2 LAMBETH PALACE ROAD; LAMBETH NORTH UNDERGROUND): This museum tells the story of how 19th-century nursing was revolutionized by this remarkable reformer. It includes much of her own medical equipment.

Museum of Garden History (ST. MARY-AT-LAMBETH, LAMBETH PALACE ROAD; LAMBETH NORTH UNDERGROUND): Beautiful exhibits and formal gardens grace a disused church and churchyard. Captain Bligh, skipper of the ill-starred *Bounty,* is buried in the old churchyard.

Darwin's Grave: Darwin is buried in Westminster Abbey — a surprise to those who believe that his theory of evolution is anti-Christian — near the grave of Isaac Newton at the north end of the choir screen.

Chapter 17

Engineering, Computer Science, and Math

If you have the wind and legs for it, climb to any high point in the city and gaze around you. The Monument will do, or the Westminster Cathedral bell tower (no cheating by taking the elevator here), or St. Paul's wonderful dome, or the Queen's Tower at Imperial College. As you look across London in any direction, you are seeing centuries of the best of humanity's conceptual and creative genius. Just about everything you see, and much that you can't, was created by people with the vision and the guts to do more than study — people who had the courage to *do!*

Your own academic experiences have exposed you to brilliant teachers and professors, and a few complete flakes, who have tried to awaken this vision in you. The people who built this city had their imaginations stimulated in the same way, and they went out and built the London you've come to study.

In this chapter we want to examine some of the marvels of world engineering and modeling, from the work of self-taught engineers of centuries past to the newest and most innovative solutions to problems you probably didn't even know existed.

THE LONDON EXPERIENCE
Tower Bridge

Everybody recognizes the most famous bridge in the world. And most people call it by the wrong name.

The splendid Victorian bridge over the Thames at the east edge of the City is not, repeat *not*, London Bridge. A chap from Arizona made that mistake when he heard that London Bridge was for sale. He bought it, thinking he was getting Tower Bridge, but actually he ended up paying more than a million pounds for a rather nondescript bridge that stood several hundred yards upriver. The naive apparently buy bridges other than the one in Brooklyn!

No one ever accused Victorian designers and engineers of subtlety, and **Tower Bridge** alone is enough evidence to convict them of visual excess. But what magnificent excess! The consulting engineer on the project was John Wolfe Barry, son of Sir Charles Barry, whose neo-gothic Houses of Parliament is another spectacular London landmark.

For more than 1500 years there had been but a single bridge across the Thames, first a succession of wooden ones built by the Romans and later the Saxons.

But the bridge had an inconvenient tendency to rot away, to wash away, or to burn up. Finally, about the year 1200 a stone bridge was built — and well built it was: it lasted 600 years! This was the famous London Bridge. But no matter how good its engineering was, 600 years is a long time. Eventually it became so decrepit that a playful song was written about it. Perhaps you've heard of it.

London Bridge was replaced with a new structure in 1831. Today, you'll find that 19th-century bridge in Lake Havasu City, Arizona. The modern London Bridge was opened in 1973.

Where does Tower Bridge fit into all this? Well, as London grew into the world's largest city, London Bridge was jammed almost to impassability most of the time, and there were too few ferries to handle the overflow. This was a particular problem because the City was strictly religious, so all the exciting places to go — the theatres, the best taverns, even the brothels — were on the other side of the river. But it wasn't until 1750 that the second Thames bridge — Westminster Bridge, way upriver near Parliament — was opened. Those chaps from Parliament wanted to assure *themselves* of easy access to the cool hangouts, presumably.

Gradually more bridges spanned the river, but none were east of London Bridge because that's where all the docks and wharves were. A bridge farther east would block the path of ships sailing upriver to unload their wares. Unless — just unless — it were a drawbridge!

In 1884 Parliament decreed that such a bridge

would be built, and that it must have an opening at least 135 feet high and at least 200 feet wide to allow the largest and tallest ships to pass through.

More than 50 designs were submitted, as was a proposal for digging an enormous tunnel instead. In the end, however, Barry's refinement of a design by Sir Horace Jones won the day.

When Tower Bridge was opened 10 years later, it was the engineering marvel of the century, and it still ranks among the greatest bridges ever built. The draw-bridge mechanism was creative and amazingly effective.

The roadway sits atop bascules, or see-saws. Each bascule weighs 1200 tons, of which 400 tons is counterweight, making it possible to raise the bridge 86 degrees — almost perpendicular! — in only one minute.

The original mechanism and control cabin of the bridge are now open for tours for just a few pounds, and it's well worth a visit. You'll see the 30-foot-long coal-fired boilers that delivered steam to the pumping engines that produced a hydraulic pressure of 850 pounds per square inch to the driving engines that raised the bridge. Amazingly, the bridge always had more than double the necessary power available at all times. Every bit of the generating mechanism was duplicated!

In a series of recent modernizations, the steam-driven hydraulics were replaced by an electric and oil hydraulic system in 1972. In more than 80 years, the old mechanism had not failed a single time. In 1979, the roadway was replaced and reinforced, since the original bridge was built for horses and carts, not lumbering lorries. And, in 1982, the walkways high above the roadway were re-opened.

The walkways were originally conceived to allow pedestrians to cross the bridge even when it was open for ships to pass through, and elevators driven by the same hydraulic engines that powered the bascules whisked people to the top quickly. But the walkways were little used. The bridge mechanism was so quick and efficient that people just enjoyed watching the ships pass, content to wait until the bridge closed so they could cross at street level. The walkways became havens for prostitutes and footpads. Now, however, they are again well-lit and very popular, with the best imaginable views of the river.

The bridge still opens a dozen or so times a week for river traffic, but openings are scheduled in advance and published in the newspaper so commuters are not caught unawares. Originally, though, the bridge would open on demand — 600 times a month or more!

You don't have to be a civil or hydraulic engineer to appreciate the wonders of Tower Bridge, but if you are, you'll be even more awed by it than the rest of your traveling companions. But if somebody offers to sell it to you, make sure you're getting the real thing before you whip out your MasterCard.

ON DISPLAY
Thames Flood Barrier

The Thames is a tidal river, rising and falling twice each day in rhythm with the sea. This has worked to London's great benefit over the years, but there are drawbacks, too. Like floods during surge tides.

People learn to live with the little inconveniences of nature like earthquakes, hurricanes, and floods, but sometimes they get fed up enough to look for solutions. London found one.

In 1984 the Queen opened the Thames Barrier, another stunning engineering achievement. More than 1700 feet wide, the barrier has floodgates that sit on the bottom of the river but can be raised in less than three hours to a height of 65 feet to protect London from sea surges.

It's a bit of technology that's important to the city. The southeast of England is sinking at the rate of a foot per century, and high tide in the city is two feet higher than it was a century ago. Wags have suggested that the weight of all the tourists is the culprit, but more likely it's the settling of the clay on which London is built.

The best way to visit the Thames Barrier is to take a boat from Westminster Pier (75 minutes) or Tower Pier (60 minutes), but a train from Charing Cross or London Bridge stations can take you more quickly, if less scenically, if you're in a hurry to see it.

COOL CORNERS

Tunnels beneath the Thames: The difficulty of building bridges across the Thames was so great that some men inevitably turned to tunneling under it — probably the only means of getting to the other side that would be harder than building a bridge. Even we know that, and we're not engineers. We hardly think of it today as we go zipping under the river on the Tube, but a tunnel under the Thames is not to be taken for granted.

The first was attempted in 1798, but not until 1843 was there a successful effort. The **Wapping-Rotherhithe Tunnel** (ROTHERHITHE UNDERGROUND) took 18 years to build and killed 10 workers, but when it was opened to pedestrians, it was the wonder of east London. More than 50,000 people climbed down the steep spiral staircases to use the tunnel the first day it was open. Shops and market stalls were set up in the tunnel's murky darkness, and the air was foul. People soon stopped using it, and it became a den of prostitutes and thieves — who apparently moved to the Tower Bridge walkway 40 years later. By the end of the century, it was taken over by the Underground system. You can use the tunnel today, but only by riding the Tube's East London line between Shoreditch and New Cross Gate.

Another tunnel crossed the Thames from the Tower to Bermondsey. Opened in 1870, it used cable cars at first to carry traffic, but later it was converted to a pedestrian tunnel. When Tower Bridge opened in 1894, this tunnel was closed to pedestrians and it now holds pipes that carry water across the river

Today, however, there are several perfectly modern pedestrian tunnels that are well-lit, well-ventilated, and well-policed. Try the one at Greenwich or another at Woolwich, about a half-mile downstream from the Thames Flood Barrier.

St. Paul's in Miniature (CRYPT OF ST. PAUL'S CATHEDRAL; ST. PAUL'S UNDERGROUND): When the City burned to the ground in 1666, the greatest loss was the pride of London, the vast St. Paul's Cathedral. Mathematician and architect Christopher Wren was personally selected by Charles II to supervise the rebuilding. Wren handled most of the churches, including St. Paul's, himself. He produced three designs for the cathedral. The first was rejected as being too continental. The second, Wren's pride and joy, was rejected because its great dome looked too much like the dome of St. Peter's in Rome and anti-Catholic feeling in England was strong. The third was much scaled back and more traditional. This design was approved, with a royal provision that Wren could make what changes he saw as necessary during the building.

Crafty to a fault, Wren began building the third design but decided that many changes were necessary, including enlarging it to the size of the second proposal and adding that very Catholic-looking dome. The royal provision gave Wren the loophole he needed to build the church he wanted.

Wren tried so hard to persuade the cathedral chapter to adopt his second design that he went to the enormous expense of building a scale-model replica of the proposal. That replica, called the "Great Model," cost three times Wren's annual salary. It is on display in the crypt of the church and worth a visit by any designer. The model itself is a work of art and is truly humbling to anyone who has ever struggled through a drafting class. (THERE'S MORE ABOUT ST. PAUL'S THROUGH-OUT THE BOOK, BUT ESPECIALLY IN CHAPTERS 8 AND 9.)

STREET STUDY
Going Underground

Maybe we should call this section an "*Under* the Street Study," because the London Underground is as much a part of the arterial network of the city as are the surface streets. London's famous Tube system, the oldest and largest subway system in the world, is an engineering marvel. By the way, don't call the Tube a "subway." In London, a subway is an underground walkway for pedestrians. On his first trip to London, one of the authors, a slow learner, spent 20 minutes trying to find the train in a subway near Hyde Park.

The Underground is such an important part of London life that people routinely identify the area they live in or the location of an event by the name of the nearest Tube station. The Underground is one of the prides of the city.

Londoners were skeptical when the Underground was proposed in 1843. Nothing like it existed in the world, and the idea presented what seemed to be numerous insolvable problems. For example, how would you keep your customers from suffocating if you were trying to entice them to ride on your subterranean *steam* railroad? The notion of dragging trains around with windlassed cables was considered and rejected. A plan to heat water with hot bricks instead of coal-fired boilers didn't work either.

Finally an engine was developed that held smoke and steam in a tank behind the engine. Vents were placed at intervals in the street, and the engines would stop beneath these vents and discharge their tanks. You would *not* want to have been walking over those grates at the wrong time!

Ride the Metropolitan Line from Baker Street to Farringdon. Opened in 1863, this is the oldest stretch of the oldest subway in the world. It was built by the "cut and cover" method of digging a deep trench, building the rail line, roofing it over, and burying it again. Some of the old "cuts" are still open to the sky, as you'll discover around Barbican Station. Tunnels built by boring deep lines through the earth were not opened until 1890; these had been impossible to vent before electric railways became available.

Ventilation was and is a major issue in the operation of the Underground, which runs as deep as 221 feet. Earlier engineers believed the movement of the trains and the action of their pistons would move the air enough to keep it comfortable. Dead wrong! But it was nearly 40 years before serious attempts were made at ventilation. Today, 127 giant fans draw 2400 cubic meters of air into the shafts every second. The year-round temperature is 73 degrees and humidity is controlled with some 700 pumps.

The people at the **London Transport Museum** can put you in touch with groups that make excursions to some of the Tube's "ghost stations." These are Underground stations that have been abandoned because of shifting traffic and residential patterns. Some are now dark and empty, and others have been converted to other uses. The old **British Museum Station** is a red brick building at 4 Bloomsbury Court; today it is the headquarters of the Household Cavalry and the Scots Guard. **Brompton Road Station,** near Harrods department store, was used during World War II to direct anti-aircraft operations and was never re-opened as a working Underground station.

General Eisenhower used the Tube as his headquarters during World War II. **Goodge Street Station** (TOTTENHAM COURT ROAD) was the location of one of the extra-deep tunnels built during the war, well below the level of the regular station. Ike had his command post there. Few of the thousands of people who use Goodge Street Station today, however, realize it has a deeper level that is now used for storage by the British Library.

IMMERSION
London's Other Waterways

The River Thames is not the only aquatic game in town. Some of the most interesting of Britain's 2000 miles of canals skirt the city, and for a true immersion experience, you should go boating.

If you'd like to spend just a couple of hours on the water, there are several places to hitch a ride. The oldest and most popular of these concessions are probably Jenny Wren Cruises in **Camden Town** or Jason's

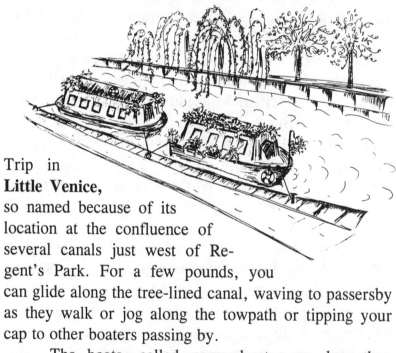

Trip in
Little Venice,
so named because of its
location at the confluence of
several canals just west of Regent's Park. For a few pounds, you
can glide along the tree-lined canal, waving to passersby as they walk or jog along the towpath or tipping your cap to other boaters passing by.

The boats, called narrowboats, are less than seven feet wide at the beam but are 40 feet or more long. They're comfortable and many families live on them full time. Thousands rent them for a week or a month for a boating holiday.

You can't help but be struck by the planning, effort, and ingenuity that went into the building of the canals. You may go through the Islington tunnel, 1000 feet long and 17 feet deep, finished in 1820. Remember that there were no suitable engines for boats in those days. They were usually pulled along by horses on the tow-path. To get through a tunnel, someone on the boat had to lie on his back on the roof of the boat and actually walk against the top of the tunnel, propelling the boat along.

You'll also enjoy the locks that allow the boats to move up and down hill. You may also encounter aqueducts, which allow canals to cross above rivers, highways, and railroads. The most impressive are out of London: if you go to Wales, see the 120-foot-high Pontcysllte Aqueduct on the Langollen Canal over the River Dee.

CROWN JEWELS

London Transport Museum (COVENT GARDEN; COVENT GARDEN UNDERGROUND): This popular Covent Garden attraction tells the story of the city's Tube, buses, taxis, and trains. There are hands-on exhibits, which include the chance to see what it's like to drive a Tube train. Plenty of attention is given to demonstrating how the city's transportation system was built. It also has one of the best gift shops of any museum in London. It's certainly the place to go for posters.

Mainline Railway Stations: These are working buildings, not museums, and studying how pedestrian, car, taxi, bus, and rail traffic are coordinated is the ultimate topological study. Most complex is the double terminus of Victoria Station, built in the 1880s to serve the southeast. Trains leave here to connect with ferries to the Continent, and London's chief bus terminal is across the street. This is also the terminus of the Gatwick Express, the special train that whisks travelers to Gatwick Airport. King's Cross Station (1867) is London's oldest terminal and one of its busiest. But *the* busiest is Waterloo. More than 180,000 people a day use this station's 2000 trains. No train, however, attracts more attention than the one using a tunnel we haven't yet talked about: the Channel Tunnel, or "Chunnel."

Called the chief engineering feat of the 20th century, this triple tunnel under the English Channel has cut the travel time from London to Paris from seven hours to just three. The Chunnel is the culmination of a centuries-old dream to connect Britain with the rest of Europe. The Eurostar train, which travels between Britain and the mainland through the Chunnel, hits speeds of nearly 200 miles per hour and simply must be experienced to be understood.

SHERLOCK SUGGESTS . . .

Battersea Power Station, south of the Thames, is an art deco masterpiece. This massive building became obsolete and now sits decaying while politicians fight over what to do with it. Suggestions have ranged from creating a vast indoor amusement park to blowing it up. Alas, time and decay are settling the issue.

The Science Museum (EXHIBITION ROAD; SOUTH KENSINGTON UNDERGROUND): The first true computer, Charles Babbage's Second Difference Engine, which he designed in 1847, is on display here in the exhibit "Computing, Then and Now." (THERE'S MORE ABOUT THE SCIENCE MUSEUM IN CHAPTER 15.)

The Canal Museum (12–13 NEW WHARF ROAD; KING'S CROSS UNDERGROUND): Discover the canal era. Here you'll learn about the herculean efforts it took to build the nationwide canal network, the locks, the boats, and the people who live and work on the canals. This new museum is one of London's best.

Chapter 18

Home Again

You're leaving London in two days. You smash into that brick wall of a thought and instead of seeing stars, the video screen in your head flashes place after place that you haven't gotten to yet, places you intended to go again, things you haven't done, and things you want to do again. You want to go up inside Tower Bridge. You never made it back to Westminster Abbey. You promised yourself you'd see a cricket match. You're a communication student and never went to the Museum of the Moving Image. How, as an English major, can you ever look your advisor in the face and admit you didn't see a Shakespearean performance at the reconstructed Globe? You promised to telephone that British student whom you met in the Fitzroy Tavern two weeks ago. Time is running out!

No matter how greedily you have soaked up London, this moment will come. Don't let "Gotta Fit It All

In" anxiety spoil your final hours abroad. The key is accepting that some things must stay undone, some places unseen. As the date of departure nears, choose a few things to brighten your remaining days and leave others as lures to draw you back. Many of you will come back to London. You'll be older, at least a little. As for wiser, who can say? You'll come back, if your circumstances allow you to, because you've developed an attachment to this place that is perhaps difficult to put into words and because you'll want to rediscover a little of the magic from this episode of your life.

The magical aspect of your study-abroad experience may become apparent when your plane takes off from Gatwick or Heathrow and you settle into your seat and reflect on what you've done. For most of you, however, perspective will come when you are back home and into your routine. After you've been back awhile, those aspects of home that you thought about often while traveling — things like eating a home-cooked meal, sleeping in your own bed, wearing different clothes, seeing your old friends — lose much of the luster that absence added. Of course, you are delighted to be back home, and you probably appreciate it more than ever. But, inevitably, your thoughts will begin to return to London, to the people you met while studying abroad, to the experiences you had.

Your time abroad went by in a blur. You saw and did so much that you could hardly absorb it all. Your return home or to school unlocks the door of reflection. So many things will elicit comparisons to your other reality. You may bump into someone and say *Sorry* instead of *Excuse me*. You might order "chips" at the restaurant and look askance at the waiter when he fails to bring you french fries. You're sitting in your car and the announcer on WXYZ says: *There's an 80% chance of rain today in the Miami Valley. The barometric pressure is falling, and the winds are out of the south-southeast at 15 miles per hour. Dense clouds will cover the Miami Valley in the morning, but the skies will improve to partly cloudy in the afternoon and clear by evening.* You smile as you endure the litany of useless weather details, recalling the concise BBC Radio One weather report in which the announcer said simply: *And now for the weather. . . . It's raining.*

Cultural comparisons big and small, consequential and inconsequential, flow freely in those first few weeks back in your homeland. One of the most useful aspects of being abroad is that it helps you to better understand your own culture, to examine why things are the way they are, to think about what you like and what you don't like about your society, and to reflect on how these forces have shaped your attitudes. Nobody counts on this as part of their travel experience, but this cultural and personal examination inevitably happens. Maybe you should petition your school for an extra credit! You probably never thought that the learning, that the cross-cultural explorations would continue after you re-entered your home territory.

Does the experience of studying abroad *change* you? Probably, but to boil the experience down to that oft-asked question somehow misses the point. Everything that you do or that is done to you has the potential to change you, but study abroad acts as a catalyst for growth, both intellectual and spiritual. You learn not just about Britain and its connection to your academic interests, but also about yourself. Besides, as we've maintained all along, studying abroad is *fun*.

Enough said!

And don't forget,
for updates to this book, check our Web site at

http://www.as.udayton.edu/com/faculty/student.htm

Index